The Life and Writings
of the Historical Saint Patrick

The Life and
Writings of the Historical
SAINT PATRICK

R. P. C. Hanson

The Seabury Press · New York

1983
The Seabury Press
815 Second Avenue
New York, N.Y. 10017

Library of Congress Cataloging in Publication Data

Hanson, R. P. C. (Richard Patrick Crosland), 1916–
  The life and writings of the historical Saint Patrick.

  Bibliography: p. 127
  Includes index.
  1. Patrick, Saint, 373?–463? 2. Christian saints—Ireland—Biography. I. Title.
BR1720.P26H36 1983   270.2′092′4 [B]   82-5861
ISBN 0-8164-0523-9   AACR2
ISBN 0-8164-2457-8 pbk

Contents

Introduction

I / The Historical Background to St. Patrick's Life

Patrick is one to whom posterity has been both generous and unfair; generous because it has heaped upon him many honors—that of becoming the patron saint of Ireland, that of being everywhere a symbol of Ireland itself and of Irish Christianity, the attribution to him of miraculous powers and enormous success; unfair because in the process of glorifying Patrick posterity has totally obscured his real lineaments, his real character, his real significance. The conventional picture of St. Patrick presents him as a modern bishop with miter and pastoral staff, banishing snakes from Ireland, teaching the doctrine of the Trinity by the example of the shamrock, overcoming the opposition of the High-King of Ireland, holding familiar concourse with a guardian angel, climbing Croagh Patrick in Co. Mayo to commune with God on the top, revisiting Mount Slemish in Co. Antrim where he is supposed to have spent an earlier period of captivity. It has represented him as the product of a Gallic education in Auxerre or Lérins, the legate of a papal mission.

Not a single one of these details is historical: miters were not invented for at least 500 years after Patrick's day. The story of his banishing snakes was concocted about three hundred years after his death, that of his teaching by means of the shamrock about a thousand years after his time. There was no High-King of Ireland in his day; the colorful story of his encounter with King Loeghaire at Tara is sheer fiction. He spent a captivity in Ireland indeed, but not on Mount Slemish. The angel Victor is the confused corruption of the name of a man whom he once mentions as having seen in a dream. He did not climb Croagh Patrick, he was not educated in Gaul, he was not sent to Ireland by the bishop of Rome. All the exciting and glamorous features that tradition has attached to Patrick must be removed if we wish to know what he was really like. And yet the

1

historical St. Patrick is more interesting and more worth studying than all these later gaudy additions.

It is incontrovertible that Patrick was British, born in Britain of British parents. He tells us so himself in his surviving works and everything else that we know about him confirms the truth of his words. But we must remember that, though British, he was not English. Patrick's Britain was pre-Anglo-Saxon Britain, Britain of the fourth and fifth centuries A.D., Roman and sub-Roman Britain, an island which in his day would have written its name in Latin (for British, Patrick's native language, was never written down) as *Britanniae*, "the Britains," not the British Isles but the British provinces. In order to understand Patrick's life we must look at the political framework in which it was lived, the late Roman Empire.

By the second century A.D. the Romans had succeeded in establishing the largest Empire yet known in the Western world. It comprised all the countries bordering on the Mediterranean and most of Western Europe. Its boundaries were fixed roughly by the Rhine, the Danube, the Euphrates, the Atlas Mountains, and the Atlantic Ocean. The whole of modern France, Spain, and Portugal, parts of modern Germany and Belgium, all of the island of Britain except for the extreme northern parts which were too wild and mountainous to control, were under its sway. Ireland the Romans had never bothered to conquer. The inhabitants of this vast area included in the Empire never manifested any long-lasting nor serious objection to Roman rule and were on the whole glad of the security and order that it imposed. There was nothing democratic and not much politically free about the Late Roman Empire, but its inhabitants were quite unused to either democracy or political freedom and did not miss them.

By the end of the second century Roman order, Roman law, and Roman civilization had acquired an enormous prestige. There had never before been an Empire that functioned as efficiently as this one. Its triumphal arches, forums, public buildings, temples, baths, and roads stretched all over Europe, the Middle East, and North Africa. It was visibly an unusually successful political enterprise.

In the third century, however, the Empire encountered some alarming shocks and failures. It was assailed by misfortunes both internal and external. Internally the Empire failed dismally to secure a stable and reliable center to its administrative machine. The succession to the position of Emperor, which had hitherto been arranged relatively peacefully, became now the prey of competing armies and adventurers. Between 211 and 284 there were at least fifteen Emperors of whom only one died in his bed. A centrifugal tendency threatened to break up the Empire into several successor states. Roaring inflation and economic and social dislocation combined with epidemics to disrupt the ordinary existence of the Roman citizen.

Externally the attacks of barbarian tribes from beyond the Rhine and the Danube and of the Persian Empire under a new and dynamic Sassanian dynasty became for periods more than the central government could cope with. However, a succession of powerful and effective Emperors at the end of the third and beginning of the fourth centuries restored the Empire to what appeared to be its former security, established a more stable gold and silver currency, and secured the Empire against its most serious threat, anarchy at the center of power. The cost of this achievement was the transformation of the position of Emperor, which had been in 180 a constitutional monarchy, into a military dictatorship whose semidivine possessor (or sometimes team of possessors) had some of the attributes of an Oriental king. He presided over an Empire which was still intact but whose political, economic, and military weakness and inefficiency were destined to bring the western half of it to complete collapse in the fifth century.

The most significant of these powerful imperial saviors of the empire was Constantine the Great (c. 270–337) who in the course of an adventurous career succeeded in eliminating all his rivals and for the last thirteen years of his life ruled as sole Emperor. Not only did he concentrate the center of power in the city of Byzantium, renamed after him Constantinople (modern Istanbul), but he finally ended the long period of hostility between the Christian Church and the Roman State, which had reached its climax in the Great Persecution pursued with greater or lesser intensity between the years 303 and 312. Constantine did not in fact formally install Christianity as the official state religion of the Roman Empire, but he gave it first toleration, and then approval, and finally positive support. With one exception, every Emperor after him was a Christian, and by the end of the fourth century—when the last man to be sole Emperor, Theodosius I, died in 395—Christianity was in fact the religion of the Roman Empire, alone regarded with favor or given financial and other support by the authorities of the state. Roman civilization and Christianity had become closely involved in the minds of most people, as they certainly were in Patrick's.

But the fifth century witnessed the swift and final collapse of more than one half of this imposing construction. Large masses of barbarian tribes from beyond the Rhine frontier surged irresistibly into the Western Roman Empire and try as they might the Roman imperial authorities could not dislodge them nor drive them back over the frontier. One by one the provinces of the West, with the significant exception of Britain, succumbed to invaders who had come not only to pillage but to settle permanently. Gaul, Spain, most of the Balkan provinces, the whole of North Africa up to the frontier with Egypt, and finally Italy itself became barbarian kingdoms settled by Goths or Suevi or Vandals or Franks, ruled by fur-clad kings who could neither read nor write instead of by Emperors or prefects in togas. By the year 470 everything west of a line drawn from north to south from Sardica (modern Sofia) to Carthage (modern Tunis) was ruled by barbarian kings. Only in the East, the former Eastern Roman Empire, gathered round its capital of Constantinople, held together to enjoy a long and illustrious history as what we now call the Byzantine Empire.

Britain had always been regarded as a possession on the extreme edge of the Roman Empire. Julius Caesar had made punitive raids into Britain in the middle of his Gallic Wars in the mid-first century B.C. But the island had not been conquered by the Romans until, in 43 A.D., troops under the Emperor Claudius began the conquest of the island. By 70 the island up to the line between the Forth and the Clyde had been subjugated. By the middle of the next century two walls—a solid stone one, with gates and forts at intervals, between the Tyne and the Solway as a base, and a line of earthworks further north between Forth and Clyde—marked the extreme northern limit of the Roman Empire.

Britain became Romanized. The country was covered by a network of Roman roads. Towns everywhere began to put up permanent buildings where none or few had been before. In the larger centers of population temples, ornamental arches and gates, baths, forums, basilicas, amphitheaters, and in the smaller places at least inns and shops and warehouses and factories, appeared. Many English country towns such as York, Lincoln, Colchester, Cirencester, Chester, Leicester, Gloucester, and Exeter, owe their beginnings to the Roman conquest. London, which was already a town, became a port of considerable importance. In several places, such as Caerleon, and at many points along Hadrian's Wall, large military establishments were created. In many places Roman villas, decorated with wall paintings and mosaics, the center of large estates, were built by wealthy Romanized Britons.

People from most parts of the Empire visited Britain as units of the Roman army, and with them a host of people in civilian occupations, grocers, craftsmen, merchants, entertainers, teachers, engineers, administrators, financial experts, slave dealers, and so on. The natural resources of the country were explored as never before, mines, fisheries, crop-raising. Harbors and forts were built and sometimes canals were cut. Latin became a spoken language in Britain, in addition to the native tongues of British (a Celtic language of which Welsh is the modern descendant) and, in places where there were settlements of Irish in western parts, Irish, and in some northern areas, Pictish; there were even a few Greek-speakers. Any writing of letters, inscriptions, and documents was of course in Latin. In course of time the original British upper classes, the aristocrats, became Romanized enough to insist upon teaching their children Latin and giving them a Roman education, and to appreciate to some extent Roman law and Roman literature. It was from these classes that Patrick sprang.

At the same time it must be emphasized that Britain always remained something of a backwater in the Roman Empire. When Juvenal the Roman satirist of the second century wishes to speak of some remote and barbarous place it is to *"Ultima Thule,"* the furthest northern part of Britain, that he refers. When Jerome in the fifth century wishes to insult his theological antagonist Pelagius, who had come from Britain, he represents him as an outlandish backwoodsman, fed on British porridge. The buildings and adornments of British Roman towns can at no point rival those of Gaul or Spain. No single British person makes any appearance in the general history of the Roman Empire until the fifth century.

Britain seems to have escaped most of the troubles that afflicted the Roman Empire during the third century, except the evils of inflation and epidemic. When, under the restoring Emperors at the end of that century, the provinces of the Empire were greatly multiplied in number and the Roman army reorganized, Britain came in for its share. It had until the middle of the third century been one province, but was divided now into several, so that it became "the Britains," which is the name that Patrick invariably gives it. At the very end of the century Britain produced a usurping Emperor for the first time, an official called Carausius who maintained an independent state for several years until early in the fourth century he was murdered by his second-in-command. This successor was himself soon deposed and executed by Constantius, one of a team of Emperors. This Constantius was the father of Constantine the Great, and it was at York in 306 that Constantius died and his son Constantine was hailed by local troops as his successor, to begin his remarkable progress towards sole imperial rule, the recognition of Christianity, and the founding of Constantinople.

It was during this fourth century that Britain began to suffer particularly from raids from barbarians—Irish (known as Scots [*Scotti*]) from the west and north, Picts from beyond Hadrian's Wall (the more northern Antonine Wall having been now long abandoned), and late in the century Saxon pirates along the southern and eastern shores. One of these barbarian raids, as we shall see, had a profound effect upon Patrick's life. Towards the end of the century yet another imperial usurper made his appearance in Britain. Like Carausius, he was no native but a military official, Magnus Maximus (383–388). Having first had himself baptized (a significant move), he crossed to the Continent with troops from Britain and maintained his imperial claims with increasing success until he met disaster and death at the hands of the Emperor Theodosius in 388.

The eruption in 407 of vast armies of barbarian invaders across the Rhine in the direction of the Pyrenees and finally beyond them produced startling results in Britain, even though none of the invaders actually landed there. Three usurpers appeared in quick succession;

the first two were murdered by their successors, and the third, who called himself Constantine, plunged, as had Magnus Maximus, into the career of an imperial claimant on the Continent, backed by whatever troops he could find in Britain, but with much less success than Magnus Maximus had met. Deserted by its local Emperor and cut off from access to the central Emperor (Theodosius' son Honorius), Britain decided on the unprecedented step of withdrawing from the Empire. The steps and the machinery whereby this was done are unknown to us, but the reasons for it are clear enough. The Empire's chief asset, the establishment of law and order, had disappeared, apparently for ever. The reliability of the imperial system was fatally damaged by the capture and sacking of Rome in that year, 410, by Alaric the Goth and his army. We can only conjecture what happened in Britain. It seems much more likely that the repudiation of Roman rule was initiated by the Romanized British aristocracy than that a popular uprising occasioned the break.

The meager information available makes it very difficult to reconstruct what Britain was like after 410, but we can be fairly sure that the country, reverting to its pre-Roman Celtic shape which had never been completely effaced, broke up into a number of successor kingdoms (whose areas were determined by long-standing tribal division) ruled by warlords who may have called themselves by the Roman name, *tyrannus*. One of them was Coroticus (or his ancestor) to whom Patrick was later to write his *Letter*.

Archaeological evidence suggests that economic decay and cultural regress followed soon upon the break with the Empire. Towns began to be deserted, villas abandoned. No more coins were minted in Britain. The Roman system of education probably collapsed. Civil war between the various warlords (a phenomenon which tended to be endemic in Celtic societies) began to appear. But in spite of all signs of decline, through force of circumstances no barbarian invasion of Britain took place. Alone among the former provinces of the Western Roman Empire it was not overrun by foreigners.

Meanwhile, Christianity had reached Britain and was growing there. British Christianity in Roman and sub-Roman Britain is a subject which has only recently begun to interest scholars. But there can be no doubt that there was a Church in Roman Britain. Christianity did not first reach Britain when the missionaries from Columba's Iona began to penetrate into Northumbria towards the end of the sixth century nor when Augustine reached Canterbury from Rome in 597. Christianity had reached Britain long before, perhaps as long as four centuries before. A fragment of a cryptogram scratched on a sherd of pottery was found by archaeologists of the University of Manchester in 1978 in a site from the old Roman town of *Mamucium* (part of modern Manchester). If we can regard this as Christian, then we can conclude that Christianity had reached Britain as early as the end of the second century, the period to which the stratum in which this sherd was found can be dated. The Christian provenance of this cryptogram is highly likely, though not certain.

Even if we had no archaeological evidence to assist us, however, we can be sure of the existence of British Christianity in Roman times from literary evidence alone. From Gildas, a Welsh monk writing in the first half of the sixth century, we know of three British martyrs: two called Aaron and Julius from Caerleon (*Urbs Legionum*) in South Wales; and one more famous, Alban, the scene of whose martyrdom was *Verulamium* (St. Albans), whose cult is also mentioned by an earlier authority than Gildas, Constantius, the biographer of Germanus of Auxerre, writing about 470. Unfortunately we cannot with certainty attribute a definite date to these martyrdoms, but they probably took place in the third century.

We also have a record of the name of a small deputation of British bishops who attended the Council of Arles in Southern Gaul in the year 314. One of them was called Eborius, bishop of York (*Eboracum*), and one was called Restitutus, bishop of London; the third, Adelfius, cannot with confidence be assigned a see because the manuscript is corrupt at this point, but it is a plausible conjecture that he was bishop of Lincoln (*Lindum*). There are a few other references to British bishops in the literature of the fourth century, and one interesting anecdote told about one of the British deputation of bishops who attended the Council of Rimini (*Ariminum*) in 359–360; there can be little doubt that a larger number than three bishops from Britain attended this (more distant) council, and this suggests that the number of the bishops, and so the number of the faithful, had increased since 314. We have noted as significant (see above, p. 6) that the usurping Emperor Magnus Maximus took care to be baptized in Britain before he made his bid for imperial rule in 383. It is much more likely that this is a testimony to the prestige of the Church in Britain than to the piety of Magnus Maximus.

Archaeology has a way of throwing unexpected shafts of light upon obscure periods of history, and sometimes archaeological finds seem at first to do no more than make the darkness visible. This is the impression we gain when we try to date the important Water Newton find made in 1975. This was the discovery of a fairly large cache of silver and gold objects carefully put away in a pot buried in a field near Water Newton in Northamptonshire. As well as the large pot which contained the objects there were a silver jug beautifully chased, a cup with handles, a dish, several triangular votive plates (one with an inscription), a gold disc, a spoon, and some other objects. The inscription and the decoration on the dish and the jar and on most of the other objects were unmistakably Christian. The jug's design suggested similar patterns to be dated to the third century, but the objects could just as well have been hidden in the fourth century after being in use for some time.

The problem of dating this find more exactly is therefore a teasing one. Were they deliberately buried in the first decade of the fourth century when, under the orders of the persecuting Emperor Diocletian, Christian Churches were pulled down and their contents destroyed? But then why were they not retrieved when the persecution was over? Were they buried by people of the Christian Church in the nearby small Roman town of *Durobrivae* during the very serious disturbances of the year 367, when Picts and Scots conspired with local troops to pillage and sack a large part of Roman Britain? And were those who buried this church silver unable to retrieve it because they had left the country or had been killed? Whatever the answers to these questions, the Water Newton find testifies to the existence of a Christian church building in the vicinity, probably in *Durobrivae*—because these objects could only have come from a church—and to some affluence among the Christians there who could dedicate such expensive donations.

In recent years it has in fact been possible by the aid of archaeology to identify several sites in Britain where a Christian place of worship certainly or very probably existed in Roman and sub-Roman times. The most interesting of these is perhaps Lullingstone near Otford in Kent where excavation upon a Roman villa has revealed the existence in the late fourth or early fifth century of a small suite of rooms in one wing of the villa deliberately adapted to Christian worship. The remains of paintings on the walls of this place have been reconstructed enough for us to identify two large emblems called Chi Rho (thus ☧ , the first two letters of the name "Christ" in Greek) surrounded by a wreath. It has also been possible to reconstruct much of one of a series of figures depicted on one wall: it is of people, clothed in beautiful, brightly-colored garments, standing in prayer. This was no doubt an estate chapel, available for the Christians who worked on the villa's property as well as for the people who lived in the villa.

Another Roman villa of the fourth century in Hinton St. Mary in Somerset has yielded a large mosaic on one floor, completely intact (now transported bodily to the British Museum in London and on show there), the central roundel of which displays the bust of Christ. This may have served as the floor of the villa's estate chapel. Another similar mosaic, unmistakably Christian by reason of the Chi Rho sign found in it, was once to be found in a Roman villa in Frampton in Dorset. The site of a Christian Church has been identified in the middle of the Roman town of *Calleva* (modern Silchester) in Hampshire, and it has even been suggested that this was the see town of a diocese. It is highly likely that traces of a Christian church of the Roman era can be found in Icklingham in Suffolk. We have seen (above p. 9) that there is a strong probability that the vessels of the Water Newton find came from a Christian church at *Durobrivae*. Conjectures of a greater or lesser probability have identified early Christian churches at Canterbury, Colchester, Richborough, Dorchester, Littlecote Park in Wiltshire, Stone-by-Faversham in Kent, and West Hill, Uley, in Gloucestershire. It is inconceivable that there were not Christian churches at London and York and St. Albans but no traces of them have yet been found.

In the fifth century, while Christianity was experiencing in the rest of Western Europe the agonies and dislocation resulting from the collapse of the Roman Empire, the British Church appears to have enjoyed a time of relative calm, prosperity, and expansion, at least during the first half of the century. For the first time individual people of the British Church figure prominently in the history of the Church: Pelagius, Augustine's opponent in a famous controversy, who had been living in Rome as an ascetic and preacher for some years before the controversy began in the early years of the fifth century; Faustus who after spending several years in the monastery of Lérins off the coast of France near Nice became bishop of Riez and a well-known preacher and ecclesiastical politician (c. 408–c. 490); Fastidius, a more shadowy figure, who is said to have been a British bishop who during this century wrote one or two works which had some circulation, though they have not survived.

We hear also, through the later Anglo-Saxon scholar Bede and some other sources, of Ninian, who evangelized in southwest Scotland during the first half of the fifth century and whose name is associated with Whithorn in modern Wigtownshire. He may have been deliberately sent and financed by the British Church as Patrick was sent and financed. Britain indeed after about 420 obtained a reputation for harboring the views of Pelagius after the death of that much-challenged teacher, so much so that Germanus, the famous bishop of Auxerre in France (fl. 418–448), made two separate visits to Britain, in 429 and in 444 or 445, in order to suppress the heresy there. His biographer Constantius gives us detailed but historically unreliable accounts of both visits. As we shall see (below, p. 61) it is certain that Coroticus, the recipient of Patrick's *Letter*, was a Christian, as were his soldiers, and probably a king or *tyrannus* of the kingdom of Strathclyde in western Scotland, with his headquarters on the Firth of Clyde; this suggests that the evangelizing activities of the British Church had extended by the middle of the fifth century far beyond Hadrian's Wall. We meet in the correspondence of Sidonius Apollinaris, a Gallic litterateur and bishop (c. 423–c. 480), an interesting person called Riochatus who was certainly a Briton and a monk, and who may have been a bishop among that considerable number of Britons who emigrated from their native land to northwest Gaul soon after the middle of the fifth century.

We shall learn more about the British Church from Patrick, who is the first British ecclesiastic whose writings have come down to us, about the "Rule of Faith" of that Church, its attitude towards monasticism, and its attachment to the Bible. But we can say with some confidence that even without the help of Patrick it is possible to envisage the British Church as successful and expanding up to the middle of the fifth century. After that the situation of the Church and

the history of Britain itself become obscure and very difficult to trace
with any confidence.

It should be noted that there certainly were Christians in Ireland
before Patrick arrived there as bishop. Prosper of Aquitaine wrote a
Chronicle mainly concerned with Church history covering the period of Popes Celestine (423–432), Sixtus III (432–440), and Leo I
(440–461), and in it he tells us that in the year 431 "Palladius was
ordained and sent as first bishop to the Irish who believed in Christ
by Pope Celestine," and not only does he refer to this event again in
a later work, but we know that he was working as Celestine's secre-
tary in 431; we can therefore be quite certain of this fact. Prosper
tells us nothing of how Palladius fared in Ireland, nor does he, nor
any other ancient authority till the year 632, mention Patrick.

II / St. Patrick's Career

Although there is no doubt that Patrick was a real historical character, and although we have two pieces of writing from his hand which
tell us much about himself, the reconstruction of his life has always
been, and still is, a matter of extraordinary difficulty. In order to
unravel the complex web of theories and reconstructions which the
centuries have knitted round his name, it is advisable first to list the
literary sources which give us, or which have been alleged to give
us, information about him. They can be divided into three classes.

1. Works written by Patrick or attributed to him.
2. Later lives of Patrick.
3. Mentions of Patrick in the Irish *Annals*.

Works Written by Patrick or Attributed to Him

First in this list must be mentioned two works which can be regarded as indisputably from Patrick's pen, though of which more will

be said later (see below, pp. 18–35). The earlier in time of the two is his *Letter to Coroticus*. The title is modern because the manuscripts in which the *Letter* appears do not give it any consistent name. It is a short letter written to Coroticus and his soldiers who have just attacked a number of men and women recently baptized by Patrick, killing some and carrying the rest off to be sold as slaves to the Irish and the Picts. The *Letter* excommunicates those to whom it is addressed and demands repentance and reparation. It is in Latin. Because it is earlier in time it is translated first in this book. The second work is one nearly three times as long, also in Latin, called the *Confession*, a name which Patrick himself gives it in the last sentence; it is written towards the end of his life, and is an acknowledgment to God of the goodness which he has shown to Patrick throughout the whole extent of that life. It is scarcely necessary to say that these two documents are of the highest importance for reconstructing Patrick's career.

Next come three short sayings in Latin attributed to Patrick under the title of "Sayings of Patrick" *(Dicta Patricii)*. One of them is certainly his because it is a brief extract from his *Letter* (see below p. 73), with the words "Thanks be to God" *(Deo gratias)* added to it. The other two, on the other hand, do not recall either Patrick's style or vocabulary and other internal evidence seems to place them in a later age than his, perhaps the seventh century or later. Some fragments of what are supposed to be letters of Patrick (also in Latin) are suspiciously like much later hagiographical material (that is, the stuff of medieval saints' lives) and seem to have been produced to suit the ecclesiastical politics of the seventh or eighth centuries.

Two interesting Latin documents purport to be the decisions of synods of clergy, including Patrick, held during his lifetime, called respectively the *Synodus I S. Patricii* and the *Synodus II S. Patricii*. The first has been held by some scholars to be genuine, at least in parts. The particular rules it lays down seem to imply a Church and an Ireland when paganism has not been eliminated and a normal diocesan organization of territorial dioceses ruled by bishops was in force, rather than a Church almost wholly dominated by a monastic structure, which was the state of affairs in Ireland perhaps as early as the end of the sixth century. But several points tell against attributing these synodal decisions to a council which really met during Patrick's lifetime; the most important are that Patrick in his authentic works gives no sign at all of working alongside other bishops, whether consecrated by him or not; in fact his words strongly suggest that there were no other bishops at least in the parts of Ireland where he evangelized. A synod of bishops with Patrick among their number in Ireland seems therefore unlikely. The other point is that it is evident from the material in these canons (i.e., rules made by a Church Council) that the Christian clergy have by now been fitted into the complex system of ancient Irish society, whereas it is virtually certain from Patrick's two genuine works that this adjustment had not taken place when he wrote. He, presumably with his clergy, was an outcast. The second "Synod of St. Patrick" is obviously a later compilation whose provisions apply to a later period (perhaps the seventh century) and whose authenticity nobody today defends.

Three poems complete the list of works attributed to Patrick or associated with him. The first is called the *Hymn of St. Secundinus*. It is a Latin eulogy of Patrick in the form of an acrostic in accented, not quantitative, metre. From about the year 800 (*Martyrology of Oengus*) it has been attributed to one of the bishops alleged by later tradition to have accompanied Patrick to Ireland, Secundinus. It shows considerable acquaintance with Patrick's *Confession*. If there was a Secundinus who accompanied Patrick to Ireland, he died, according to the Irish *Annals,* several years before Patrick did; this makes it unlikely that he could have read the *Confession,* composed at the end of Patrick's life. Further, it is unlikely that Patrick, who, as we shall see (below, p. 37) was abnormally self-deprecatory, would have tolerated the composition of a hymn about himself full of unstinted admiration, and even less likely that he would have (on an alternative hypothesis) borrowed phrases from the eulogy written by his dead friend to include in the *Confession*. Finally, we have already observed that it is wholly unlikely that Patrick had any fellow bishop with him in Ireland. This *Hymn of St. Secundinus* must be a composition later than Patrick's day by a few centuries.

The next poem is a very famous one, the "Breastplate of St. Patrick," known to millions of Christians throughout the world in the version of it made by Mrs. C. F. Alexander, "I bind unto myself today," found in the hymnbooks of almost all denominations. Its original is in Irish, and it was known in the Middle Ages as the *Lorica* (of which "Breastplate" is a translation). Its form, an incantation against various dangers, especially those arising from magic, is paralleled elsewhere in the Celtic churches and may have had a pagan prototype. It is a fine piece of work, but it is almost certainly not by St. Patrick because the experts in ancient Irish tell us that its language belongs to a stage of the development of that tongue several centuries after Patrick's day.

Finally, there is a poem in Irish called the *Hymn of Fiacc*, or, as an Irish title, *Genair Patraic*, attributed to Patrick in one of the later Lives of Patrick which we shall discuss presently. Once again, Patrician authorship of this piece is ruled out by the type of ancient Irish which it displays, a type considerably later than that of the fifth century, perhaps as late as the eighth century.

This brief account of the literature actually written by or wrongly attributed to Patrick may suggest to the reader that posterity has been very ready to assign to Patrick matters which in fact belong to much later ages.

Later Lives of Patrick

There are several medieval Lives of Patrick, but the only two which have any claim to historical authenticity are those found in the *Book of Armagh*, a collection of documents transcribed in Armagh in the year 807 and now in the Library of Trinity College, Dublin (though other manuscripts of the first of the two are extant). The first of these is by a man called Muirchú Maccu Machteni (usually known as Muirchú) who wrote in the second half of the seventh century or possibly at the very beginning of the eighth, in Latin. It purports to supply many historical details about Patrick: his mother's name, his ecclesiastical education at Auxerre in Gaul under Germanus, his mission to Ireland from Auxerre, his consecration as a bishop not by Germanus but by a mysterious character Amathorex (who may be a confused reminiscence of Germanus' *predecessor* in the see of Auxerre, Amator). Muirchú has Patrick disembark, after the failure of Palladius' mission, in Wicklow in the southeast of Ireland and then journey by sea to Co. Antrim in the northeast where he seeks the place where he is alleged to have spent his captivity in Ireland, Mount Slemish, and his former master Miliucc. He narrates also the famous story of Patrick's encounter with Loeghaire, High-King of Ireland, at Eastertime on the hill of Tara in Meath and his success in lighting with impunity the Easter fire against the king's orders. He confines Patrick's activity, however, mainly to the northeast of Ireland and describes the foundation of Armagh as his see.

The other life is by a man called Tirechán, and is known only from the *Book of Armagh*. It gives us details about Patrick's other names and agrees with Muirchú in placing his captivity in Mt. Slemish. It describes him as spending a long time traveling in Gaul, in Italy, and in the "isles of the Tyrrhenian sea" and assigns to him a residence of thirty years on an island called *Aralensis* (? Lérins). He arrives in Ireland, according to Tirechán, accompanied by an imposing crowd of bishops, priests, and clergy and ministers of every sort. Tirechán brings him into contact with Loeghaire on Tara at Easter also and then conducts him on a tour around the whole of Ireland. So far Tirechán's narrative is in Latin, but in one of a number of appendices (called *Additamenta*) written partly in Irish and partly in Latin, he describes a stay in the town of *Olsiodora* (? Auxerre) by Patrick.

Tirechán's work must be placed in the second half of the seventh century. It can confidently be connected with the ecclesiastical politics of his day, when the monastery and see of Armagh were claiming jurisdiction over all other churches in Ireland, in opposition to the powerful monastic connection which appealed to the authority of Columba. Armagh was using the name of Patrick, associated with Armagh, as its most potent propaganda weapon. These two Lives are full of improbable miracles in the tradition of Irish hagiography, but they appear sober and restrained in comparison with a later compilation, probably put together between 859 and 901, called the *Vita Tripartita*, in which folklore and pious imagination have run riot; among other embellishments of the earlier story, this work brings Patrick to visit Rome in the time of Pope Celestine, to study there under Germanus, to spend a further period under Germanus at Auxerre, and, to finish things off properly, to live for a period as a monk at Tours under Martin (ob. 397)! It must by now have become obvious to the reader that Patrick's life has become subject to a large amount of hagiographical embroidery and fictitious enhancement.

Mentions of Patrick in the Irish *Annals*

Historians of medieval Ireland have at their disposal a series of *Annals* compiled in Irish monasteries or those under Irish influence and carried on from year to year, and sometimes, when one monastery could no longer continue the series, taken up by another, over a considerable period of time, in some cases reaching as late as the sixteenth century. They have such names as the *Annals of Ulster*, the *Annals of Lough Cé*, the *Annals of Inisfallen*, the *Annals of Clonmacnois*, the *Annals of Connacht*, the *Annals of the Four Masters*, and as well the *Chronicles of the Picts and Scots*. These *Annals* all purport to give several details of Patrick's career. They unanimously place his arrival as a bishop in Ireland in the year 432, the year after Palladius' arrival. They give details of the year of his birth, his captivity in Ireland, his revisiting the country as a bishop, his "confirmation" as bishop by Pope Leo I, the names of his episcopal companions, his revision of the Laws of Ireland. But they differ between themselves about the date of his birth and are greatly confused about the date of his death. Some place his death in or around 461, but others postpone it to 489 or 496. Mention can also be found in some of the *Annals* of a "second Patrick" or an "ancient Patrick" distinct from the other, and their suggestion that two Patricks existed is echoed by the *Martyrology of Oengus*, the *Hymn of Fiacc*, and one or two other medieval texts.

Ever since the sixteenth century scholars of different nationalities and backgrounds—Irish, German, French, American, Canadian, and even a few English—have endeavored to construct out of this medley of later tradition a consistent and convincing account of Patrick's biography. An interesting book could be devoted solely to the history of Patrician scholarship and how it reflects the diverse national and other prejudices and motives of the scholars who have engaged in it. But several considerations must make the modern reader pause before he plunges into the thickets of tradition about Patrick intent upon emerging with a plausible account of the saint's career won from the jungle.

There is a significant gap between the fifth century when Patrick lived and the seventh when people first begin to write about him, quite long enough for any surviving oral tradition about Patrick to have become corrupted by the tendency towards legend and wonder so richly evident in Irish hagiography. Investigation has shown that no surviving set of *Annals* can have been begun earlier than about the year 740, so that entries dealing with events earlier than that can only be based on standard Church histories (e.g., those of Eusebius, of Jerome, and of Prosper which do not mention Patrick), fallible popular memory, and sheer invention. There is no evidence in all this mass of tradition of the existence of an early authentic connected account of Patrick's life, but plenty of signs that the Patrick legend or legends were used in the cause of ecclesiastical policy. Later conditions, such as the existence of somebody claiming to be a High-King of Ireland and perhaps the establishment of a powerful see of Armagh, were freely read back into the age of Patrick. The desire to connect Patrick with important people who were known to have lived about his time, such as Martin, Germanus, and Pope Leo I, is obviously present in the minds of the writers and their sources. Even the date assigned to Patrick's arrival in Ireland as a bishop, 432, about which there is entire unanimity among biographers and annalists alike, can be accounted for by their desire to see Patrick as an immediate successor to Palladius whose date Prosper had fixed securely.

St. Patrick's Career in the Light of his Authentic Writings

It is therefore advisable for scholars investigating the life of Patrick to adopt a clear and consistent critical method which shall owe as little as possible to the hazards of picking and choosing among the doubtful mass of later stories about Patrick, and shall concentrate primarily upon the two sources of information that are contemporary with Patrick, that is the evidence of his own authentic writings and the evidence of contemporary history and convention and practice as far as we can reconstruct them. This method drastically reduces the evidence available to us but is not impracticable and will secure to us a more reliable picture of the man and his age. It is the method that is followed in this book.

The general outline of Patrick's career is easily established and has never been seriously disputed. He was born in Britain of British upper-class or aristocratic parents. When he was nearly sixteen he was captured by Irish pirates who carried him off to Ireland where he spent six years as a slave tending sheep. He then escaped from Ireland. Later he returned to Ireland as a bishop and spent the rest of his life evangelizing in Ireland, where he died. But when we wish to probe further than this and to discover more exact details of his life we run into problems.

We shall first ask, "Where was Patrick born?" He tells us himself that his home was a place called *Bannavem Taberniae* (*Conf*.1). But we can be certain neither of where this place was nor of the exact form of its name. It is perfectly possible that Patrick originally wrote *Bannaventa Berniae* and that later copyists (who can have known little or nothing of the place to which he was referring) corrupted the name. We know many of the place-names of Roman and sub-Roman Britain, but none of them are like *Bannavem Taberniae*. On the other hand, we know of several places which were called simply *Venta* (as Caerwen in South Wales and Caister-by-Norwich), and one which was called *Bannaventa* (modern Daventry in Northamptonshire) and another called *Glannaventa* (Ravenglas in Cumbria) and another called *Banna* (Bewcastle, just north of Hadrian's Wall). There are difficulties about them all. Anywhere near the east coast of Britain is ruled out because Irish raiders would not attack the east coast when they were within a few miles of the west coast, and anywhere at all far inland would be made virtually inaccessible to them by the dense forests which at that time covered much of Britain. *Glannaventa* was one of the headquarters of the Roman fleet, which would therefore be a most improbable place for pirates bent on spoil to attack. Places near Hadrian's Wall face the difficulty that there is very little evidence for the existence of villas there in late Roman and sub-Roman Britain, yet Patrick's home certainly was a villa owned by Calpornius, his father (see Commentary, p. 77). We shall probably never know exactly where Patrick's home was. All we can say is that it must have been near the western or the southwestern coast of Britain to be exposed to raids from Irish pirates and if we are to be guided by the statistics of villas so far discovered it is more likely to have lain in the south than in the north of the country.

If we next ask the question, "When was Patrick born?" we find
that satisfactory evidence for an answer is surprisingly scarce. That
the greater part of Patrick's life lay in the fifth century we need not
doubt. The later tradition can assure us of that at least. He cannot
have lived before the reign of Constantine the Great who died in
337, because he refers to a coin called the *solidus* (*Letter* 14, see
Commentary, p. 69) first coined by that Emperor, and he can
hardly have lived later than the second half of the fifth century,
because he envisages "Romans" in Gaul living near to Franks, and
subject to raids by them (*Letter* 14, see Commentary, p. 69), a
situation which did not exist after about 485. But are we to place his
career early in the fifth century or late in it? There is virtually no
direct evidence to decide this question, and very diverse theories
have been held on the subject. Most scholars have accepted the later
tradition that he landed in Ireland as a bishop in 432, and therefore
his career must be placed wholly or largely in the first half of the fifth
century. But at least one reputable scholar has suggested that his
career should be placed earlier, bringing him to Ireland about 380
and placing his death about 430. More recently some have argued
that his career covered largely the second half of the fifth century,
and, relying on the later date given for his death in some of the
Annals, have envisaged him arriving in Ireland as a bishop about 460
and dying sometime after 490. Sometimes in putting forward this
reconstruction they have relied on the not implausible theory that
Palladius and Patricius have become confused in the tradition and
that much of what should be attributed to the life and work of Palladius has been wrongly transferred to Patrick.

I believe that this question can be answered with fair confidence;
a series of small but significant pieces of evidence all pointing in the
same direction can give us the answer. The strongest indication is
given by Patrick's own reference to the educational system that prevailed when he was growing up. Patrick was, as we shall see, abnormally conscious of the deficiencies of his own education. His capture
by the Irish pirates interrupted his education so that he missed
something which he never recovered and which many of his contemporaries, to whom he refers almost with envy, possessed. He tells us
quite specifically in the early chapters of his *Confession* what it was
that he had missed and they had gained: a capacity to write correct

and elegant Latin which would appeal to the learned; a knowledge of law; and the practice of rhetoric (see *Conf.* 9–10 and 13 especially). He even calls those whom he envies and whom in a sense he regards as his opponents, or at least as his scorners, "skilled masters of rhetoric . . . who appear to be wise and powerful in speech" (13). Now, these particular accomplishments correspond very well to those acquisitions which the third stage of Roman education was intended to confer on students. Education in the Late Roman Empire was divided into three stages, the *ludus*, where the pupils up to the age of about twelve acquired the art of reading and writing and some basic mathematical skill; the *ludus grammaticus*, where from twelve to sixteen or seventeen they learned grammar and literature; and the school of the *rhetor*, corresponding to our higher education, where they primarily studied the art of speaking persuasively and writing effectively (which meant to the Romans elegantly and rhetorically), and incidentally (because the chief arena for exercising those skills was the law-court) where they had to learn some Roman law.

The *rhetor* stage corresponds exactly to what Patrick laments that owing to his six years of captivity spent in Ireland he missed and never regained. This suggests strongly that the ordinary Roman system of education existed in Britain, and would have been inculcated in the sons of the British upper classes, when Patrick was growing up. As long as the Roman Empire in the West held together and there was money to pay teachers and a career open to talents for their pupils this type of education prevailed in Britain. But when Britain was cut off from the Roman Empire, when money no longer flowed into the country from the Continent (and archaeology assures us that it did not after about 408), when courts of Roman law and places in the Roman administration and the Roman army were no longer available, then all the evidence suggests that the Roman system of education broke down. This means that Patrick must have received his interrupted education before Britain withdrew from the Roman Empire and that during his boyhood the educational system was available to such of his contemporaries as did not have the misfortune to be captured by Irish pirates. On the basis of this argument, Patrick cannot have been born long after about 390.

With this argument another more complex but still significant series of facts fits in. Patrick tells us that his father was a deacon of the

British Church (and his grandfather a presbyter) and owned a villa (that is, an estate, not just a house) near the village where he was deacon (*Conf*.1) and also that his father was a *decurion* (*Letter* 10). A *decurion* was an official of a local town council under the administrative system of the Late Roman Empire who was responsible for raising the taxes for the imperial government in the area covered by his council, and if he could not produce the required amount from the local people he was required to make good the deficit out of his own pocket. In the later stages of the Roman Empire's history, and most of all in the fourth century, this necessity became a very great burden which, in spite of the honor which was still thought to attach to the office, wealthy members of the upper classes (who alone formed the *ordo* or council of each town or city) would at all costs try to avoid.

One hopeful way of evading this burden of taxation was to become ordained as a deacon or presbyter in the Christian Church. Constantine the Great in the first flush of his enthusiasm for the Church had emancipated all clergy from these "*curule*" burdens, as they were called (because the council could also be called the *curia*). The result was naturally a rush of wealthy upper-class people into Holy Orders. Later Emperors, supported by the most responsible of the clergy and especially by the Popes, took measures to reduce this promising taxation loophole. By the last quarter of the fourth century it was established that if a *curule* official wanted to be ordained he must surrender two-thirds of his property to a relation who would then be responsible for exacting and paying the taxes due. Calpornius, Patrick's father, therefore, ought not to have been a deacon and also a *decurion* and also the owner of a villa with a large staff. It could of course be argued that this shows that he occupied these positions after Britain had left the Roman Empire, when presumably the ban on holding both offices did not apply. But we have no evidence at all for the existence of *decurions* or municipal councils in Britain after 410, and if the movement for separation came from the upper classes, as seems likely, they would have been the last people likely to perpetuate the Roman system of taxation, as they were among its chief victims. Further, the decline of villas is very clear from the second decade of the century onwards. It is much more likely that Calpornius became a deacon in order to escape the *curule* burdens (and he would have been under no necessity to proceed further to the presbyterate to fulfil this purpose), and yet managed illegally to hold on to his ancestral property as well. Patrick suggests in more than one place that his home was not a particularly religious one (e.g., "I did not then know the true God" *Conf.* 1), and this is consistent with the view that Calpornius had become a deacon for baser motives than a conviction of God's calling. The period after the fall of Magnus Maximus in 388 and before the arrival in Britain of the last competent general to visit that island, Stilicho, some time between 395 and 399, might well have given him this opportunity. And this conclusion fits in with the other that Patrick can hardly have been born later than 390.

Consistent with this date is the conviction to be found in many places in Patrick's writings that the world and history are in their last age, that everything will end in Judgment Day soon. He links this with his evangelistic activity in Ireland. Ireland, to a man of classical antiquity, was literally the last country on earth. It was the most westerly country in Europe; beyond it was nothing but the vast unexplored ocean stretching on to the edge of the world. Patrick was called by God to preach the gospel to the last nation in the last days. This expectation of the end of the world had been given a great impetus by the capture of Rome by Alaric in 410 and the gradual extinction of the Western Roman Empire thereafter. Such an expectation would be understandable in a man who had witnessed these unprecedented and appalling events in his youth, having been brought up in the assumption that the Roman Empire, now that it was Christian, could never collapse, since God would grant it immunity from disaster. But had Patrick been writing in the 480s or even 490s the impact of such a relatively distant event would have been less, and he would have been accustomed to an Empire which was obviously in process of dissolution.

Another small but significant point is his reference to the gold coin *solidus* (*Letter* 14). After 410 no formal payment of salaries to officials or soldiers would have been made by the Imperial Government. No coins of any sort were minted after that date in Britain; Ireland was destined to see its first coins produced locally only in the tenth century when the commercially minded Danes settled down and founded towns. The *solidus* would have been a strange exotic coin to the Britons of 470 or 480, whereas if Patrick was referring to *solidi* some thirty or forty years after 410 it would not have sounded as strange to his readers. Again, his references to the "Romans" and the Franks in the *Letter* 14 seem to suit the period 440–460 rather than a time several decades later when there were no enclaves of Romanized Gauls maintaining their independence among the barbarian kingdoms (see Commentary on this chapter, p. 69).

Finally we may note that although the history of Britain in the second half of the fifth century is obscure and tangled, especially as related to us in the vague and confusing prose of the sixth-century British writer Gildas, most of the evidence suggests that internal strife and the necessity of coping with the warlike activities of invading Picts and rebellious Saxon mercenaries and other bodies of Saxons determined to settle in the southeast of the island would have made the British Church's enterprise of sending Patrick as a missionary to Ireland and continuing to finance him while he was there much more difficult than it would have been had his mission been undertaken at an earlier period from about 430 to about 460.

Some scholars have attempted to date Patrick by the tyrant Coroticus against whom he wrote his *Letter*. Others have tried to date Coroticus by Patrick. The second enterprise is more hopeful than the first, because historical references to Coroticus, though not wholly lacking, are very uncertain, consisting of Welsh and Irish genealogies and a heading to a chapter in Muirchú's *Life* which does not appear in the *Book of Armagh*. We have to choose between two men of the same name, one of them the son of a British chief who is alleged to have moved with his men from an area on the north shore of the Firth of Forth (modern Fife) to the north of Wales, where he and his sons carved out a principality for themselves, now reflected in modern Cardiganshire ("Ceretic"-shire). The other is thought to have been king or tyrant of Strathclyde, an undoubtedly historical British kingdom whose center was Dumbarton on the Firth of Clyde. On the whole it is preferable to identify Patrick's Coroticus with the king of Strathclyde, because he would have been in a much better position to sell his captive Christian neophytes to the Picts than would a ruler situated in North Wales.

The alternative, later dates attached to Patrick (which would bring him to Ireland as a bishop about 460 and have him die there about 490) are favored in certain scholarly circles today. However they are not supported by any evidence in Patrick's writings, but rather rest upon not very convincing external evidence. The theory demands that much attributed to Patrick happened in fact to Palladius earlier and not to Patrick later, adduces some references in the *Annals* to friends and disciples of Patrick who may be historical figures who met their deaths in the second decade of the sixth century, and rests on a hypothesis, which can only be called farfetched, that one of the series of *Annals* may have incorporated material from a hypothetical series kept in Columba's monastery of Iona which might have retained a genuinely historical memory of Patrick's death some eighty years after it had taken place. This reconstruction suffers from the weakness which has too long afflicted Patrician scholarship; it ends by discounting internal evidence in Patrick's writings in favor of later tradition about him.

I conclude therefore with some confidence that it is sounder to place Patrick's career mainly in the first half of the fifth century, to envisage him as born about 390, as enduring his captivity in Ireland from about 405 to 411, and as returning to Ireland as a bishop about 430 and dying about 460.

We next must ask, "Where in Ireland did Patrick spend his captivity?" Later tradition, as represented by the Lives and *Annals,* is unanimous in answering, in Mount Slemish in Co. Antrim, in the extreme northeast of Ireland. Until recently reconstructions of Patrick's life have always taken this information as indisputably true. But a careful consideration of Patrick's own words should cause us to pause before lightly accepting this tradition. He tells us (*Conf.* 17) that the boat which finally conveyed him away from Ireland after he had escaped from his master was about two hundred miles away from the scene of his captivity. Even if Patrick was intending to escape from Ireland to Gaul, which, as we shall see, is virtually ruled out by Patrick's own words, he would not have needed to travel two hundred miles to find such a craft, presumably on the southeast coast somewhere, starting from the neighborhood of Mount Slemish in Co. Antrim. But in fact it is almost certain that when he escaped from his master Patrick was not making for Gaul but for his native Britain. The Message which he received in a vision just before he ran away said, "You have been right to fast because you will soon return to your country" (*Conf.* 17); Patrick's native country (and that is what the Latin word *patria* means) was Britain. He never gives us the faintest inkling that it was not to Britain that he returned. If therefore, as the evidence compels us to conclude, he was making for Britain, it would have been ludicrous for him to travel two hundred miles in order to find a ship to bring him to Britain; twenty or thirty miles would have sufficed.

It seems wholly unlikely then that Patrick set out from Co. Antrim. And in fact we can be pretty sure that he discloses the place where he spent his captivity when in *Conf.* 23 he tells us of a vision which he had many years after he had escaped and returned to Britain. In this he sees a letter with the heading "The Cry of the Irish" and immediately afterwards hears "the voice of those who were by the wood of Voclut which is near the Western Sea," and what they were saying was "Holy boy, we are asking you to come and walk among us again." The clear impression which must be created in the mind of anyone who reads this without being blinded by a preoccupation with the later tradition is that the people of the Wood of Voclut were the people among whom Patrick had spent his captivity; the impression is strengthened by the fact that they call him "Holy boy," a nickname he might well have acquired while he was among them because he tells us that he lived as pious a life as he could in captivity (*Conf.* 16), and by the use of the word "again" (*adhuc*, which in the late, colloquial Latin used by Patrick means "again" and not "up till now" as it would in literary Latin).

The reference to this place being near the Western Sea is particularly significant. Patrick was writing his *Confession* in Ireland; the "Western Sea" could only mean the Atlantic Ocean; it would be perverse to take it as the Irish Sea which lay to the east of him. Now Tirechán tells us that the Wood of Voclut lay within the district of Tirawley which covers the country just west of the border between Co. Mayo and Co. Sligo near the small town of Killala. We can here confidently rely on later tradition because place-names survive intact in oral tradition longer than any other material and because Tirechán himself, though he wrote in Armagh, came from the district of Tirawley and knew the terrain. Finally we can observe that a journey of two hundred miles after escape from his master would be much more consistent with Patrick's making his way from the northern coast of Mayo to the coast of Wicklow or Wexford, in a diagonal line right across Ireland, than with a journey from Mount Slemish to the east coast. We are driven to the conclusion that the later tradition which placed Patrick's captivity in Mount Slemish is wrong and that we must accept the plain evidence of his own words and place his captivity in Co. Mayo near the border with Co. Sligo. The people of the diocese of Killala can boast that their territory saw Patrick's captivity with much more probability than those who live near Mount Slemish in Co. Antrim.

We must next ask, "Where did Patrick receive his ecclesiastical education?" Because until recently scholars have been obsessed with the desire to include as much as possible of later tradition in their reconstructions of Patrick's life, they have tended to assume that he was prepared for ordination on the Continent and indeed dispatched to Ireland as a bishop from there. Certainly the Lives and the *Annals* give a wide range of possibilities—Lérins, Auxerre, Tours, Rome— even though their accounts may be inconsistent and their reproduction of names confused. Was he sent to Ireland by the Pope, as Palladius was? Was he a protégé of Germanus of Auxerre, who certainly visited Patrick's native land at a period in which he could have met Patrick? Two considerations, however, constitute objections to assigning a Continental education to Patrick, objections which we may without exaggeration call fatal.

The first objection arises out of the character of Patrick's Latin. This book is not written for those who can read Latin and does not give Patrick's works in their original Latin, but it is still necessary to discuss this subject, one which can readily be understood even by those who do not know Latin. From a very early point, even as early as some of the earliest scribes of the manuscripts of Patrick's works, the quality of the Latin which he wrote has puzzled and even shocked his readers. Patrick himself was well aware of his deficiencies in this respect: "Our speech and language," he says, "has been translated into a foreign tongue, as can easily be demonstrated from the savor of my writing, the extent of my education and learning" (*Conf.* 9). By this he certainly means the small extent of his education and learning and the extraordinary savor of his Latin. Indeed it is clear throughout the *Confession* that he is acutely aware of the inadequacy of his mastery of the Latin language. One might almost say that ever since Patrick wrote his friends have been trying to improve his Latin. Scribes, editors, and scholars have until very recently felt that the Latin of Patrick was unworthy of so great a saint and have tried to alter it by corrupting or emending the readings in the manuscripts of his two works.

The fact that this well-meaning but disastrous process has now stopped is due almost solely to the work of one man, the late Ludwig Bieler of University College, Dublin. Bieler, a very accomplished scholar both in palaeography and in late Latin, recognized that Patrick was writing, not literary Latin, the kind of Latin written by the great names in Latin literature—Cicero, Livy, Sallust, Quintilian, Tacitus, and among the Church Fathers, Tertullian, Hilary, Ambrose, Jerome, and Augustine—but a kind of Latin which is known as Vulgar Latin or Colloquial Latin. This was the Latin that was spoken, vernacular Latin, and it differed from literary Latin even more than spoken English differs from written English. You learned literary Latin at the school of the *rhetor*; Vulgar Latin was what you spoke, the language of soldiers, tradesmen, sailors, grooms, and slaves, the kind of Latin which was usually not written except in graffiti on walls and occasionally in epitaphs on the tombstones of humble people. It took all sorts of liberties with grammar and syntax which those who wrote literary Latin would have rigorously avoided. Its syntax was loose, its style verbose, its constructions often ungrammatical. It did not use rhetorical artifice, which was the life and soul of literary Latin. By the nature of things it does not survive in many examples of literature, but enough have come down to us for everybody to recognize, once Bieler had drawn attention to the fact, that this was the kind of Latin used by Patrick. He is indeed, though the world of Latin scholarship has hardly yet recognized the fact, one of our main sources for the Vulgar Latin of the fifth century.

But there is a further important point to be noticed about Patrick's Latin. Even in the genre of Vulgar Latin, he is not fluent. He finds it hard to express himself clearly. He is aware of this himself: "I cannot hold forth in speech to cultivated people in exact language, expressing what my spirit and mind desire and my heart's sentiment indicates" (*Conf.* 10). Patrick's Latin time and time again strikes the reader as inefficient, awkward. He gropes for words; on several occasions, as the *Commentary* will indicate, he simply fails to convey what he means and we cannot be sure precisely what he is trying to say. This was not because he was writing Colloquial Latin. We have an account written in Colloquial Latin by an intrepid and inquisitive nun called Etheria (from Aquitaine, between Gaul and Spain) of her travels in the Holy Places, for the benefit of her sisters in the convent at home. She is entirely fluent and is never at a loss for words; indeed we gain the impression that she must have struck the ecclesiastical and civil authorities in many parts of the Near East whom she was pestering with questions as a first-class bore.

To Patrick, however, Latin of any sort does not come easily. There is no other language in which he can write, but he does not write Latin easily. He has in fact never learned Latin, even Vulgar Latin, thoroughly. It does not come off his tongue. He admits so himself. We cannot attribute this inadequacy to his disuse of Latin, to the possibility that he may not have had occasion to use Latin for several years before he wrote his works. He never complains of difficulty because of not using the language. Though he does complain of difficulty in expressing himself in Latin he ascribes the difficulty more than once to lack of education. Besides, he can hardly have had no occasion for using Latin while he was a bishop in Ireland. All writing of any sort in his circumstances had to be done in Latin; as far as we know neither Irish nor British had yet been reduced to writing. In what language are we to imagine that Patrick corresponded with his friends and supporters in Britain? In what language had he written his first disregarded letter to Coroticus' men (*Letter* 3)? Patrick's trouble in writing was not lack of practice but lack of capacity.

Now, if we were to envisage Patrick as having spent many years on the Continent, in Gaul or in Rome, preparing for ordination, ministering as a deacon and presbyter or living in some monastic community, whether at Lérins or Auxerre, it is inconceivable that he would not have become fluent in Latin, quite possibly in literary Latin, but at least in Vulgar Latin. Latin would have been the only language available to him. They did not speak Gallic in Gaul any more, nor either of the other two languages which Patrick certainly knew, British and Irish. It is therefore impossible to imagine that he spent any long period on the Continent acquiring or completing his ecclesiastical education. As we shall see, he probably did pay a visit to Gaul, but he could not have spent any long period there. The state of his Latin however corresponds very well with the kind of Latin which he would have found spoken and written in the British Church. It is clear from several indications that Vulgar Latin must have been spoken in Britain as long as the Roman occupation of that country lasted and necessarily for some time after that occupation had ceased. Patrick must have learned some Latin at school before he was kidnapped; one might call it basic Latin. The rest of his Latin would have come from the kind of Latin used in a Church whose members were mostly not native speakers of Latin but which found it essential to preserve some Latin culture for the purpose of holding services, of reading and studying the Bible, and for communicating in any written form at all, while its members spoke to each other in their native British. Patrick must therefore have received his ecclesiastical formation not on the Continent but in Britain.

An eminent authority on Christian Latin, Professor Christine Mohrmann of the University of Nijmegen, has declared that Patrick could only have learned his Latin in Gaul (*The Latin of St. Patrick*, Dublin 1961). But her main reason for saying so was that she recognized that Patrick's Latin had in it a large element of Vulgar Latin, and she assumed that he could only have learned this on the Continent. She did not realize that Vulgar Latin was certainly spoken in Roman and sub-Roman Britain, as has been clearly established since she published her study of St. Patrick. She also noticed, and found it not easy to account for, a certain archaism in Patrick's Latin. A leading authority on early Britain, Professor Kenneth Jackson, whose book *Language and History in Early Britain* (Edinburgh 1953) Professor Mohrmann had apparently not read, has detected a not-dissimilar note of archaism in Latin used in Britain. We must, in short, envisage Patrick's Latin, whatever its quality, as acquired in Britain and not in Gaul.

This conclusion is strengthened by a second point. Patrick, as we shall see, is interested in Gaul, but it is perfectly clear, from his account of the events which led up to his being dispatched as a bishop to Ireland, that he was sent from Britain, not from Auxerre nor Lérins, and not from Rome. If he had been sent from Rome, there was at least one point in his review of his career when he must have mentioned the fact. He was, he tells us, seriously attacked during his period in Ireland by a delegation from Britain which questioned his right to be a bishop in Ireland (*Conf.* 26–32, see Commentary *in loc*). This is the point at which he could have defied his accusers by pointing out that he had behind him the authority of the bishop of Rome, an authority which in the fifth century was by no means to be despised, and one which had already in all probability sent one bishop to Ireland, Palladius.

But Patrick makes no mention of this at all. He refers more than once to the period just before he was sent as a bishop to Ireland (*Conf.* 32, 46) and to a very close friend of his who supported the project warmly, one to whom he had confessed a sin years before when he was about to be made a deacon (*Conf.* 27). It is inescapably obvious that this friend was in Britain and that the whole plan for sending Patrick to Ireland was agitated, whether by those who opposed or those who favored it, in Britain. Patrick writes much of his *Confession* with the British Church in mind. He feels himself obliged to account for his handling of finance, which was probably supplied from Britain, to British churchmen (*Conf.* 49–53). The internal evidence from Patrick's own writing compels us to realize that he was educated for the ministry in Britain, spent his ministry between ordination and the mission to Ireland in Britain, was in fact wholly the product of the British Church, and that the later tradition, which sends him with such imaginative abandon to Lérins or to Auxerre or to Rome or to an island in the Tyrrhenian sea, must be discounted.

We are now in a position to fill in some of the details of Patrick's career. He was born towards the very end of the fourth century, in Britain, of parents who were wealthy property-owners and probably aristocrats. "I bargained away my aristocratic status," he says (*Letter* 10). His family home was not the scene of great piety nor religious feeling, in spite of the fact that his father was a deacon and his grandfather had been a presbyter. When he was nearly sixteen he was captured by Irish pirates making a raid on his father's estate, was brought over to the other side of Ireland to a place on the edge of the Atlantic near modern Killala and employed for six years as a slave tending sheep. During that period from a state of carelessness about God he became an unusually devout convert and worshipper. After six years he managed to escape, made his way in a southeasterly direction across Ireland and at some place on the coast, probably of modern Wicklow or Wexford, was able to take ship for Britain (for the details of his journey see *Conf.* 16–23 and the Commentary).

At some point after that he was accepted for the ministry of the British Church, was trained sufficiently to be made deacon and therefore also later presbyter. While he was on a visit to Gaul his name was proposed for the task of going as a bishop to Ireland to minister to the Christians there and to convert the pagan Irish to Christianity. On his return to Britain the decision was made that he should go; he had already had experience of the Irish and no doubt could speak their language. He duly went and thereafter never returned to his native country nor to Gaul but died in Ireland among his flock without apparently having been able to arrange for another bishop to share his work nor to succeed him.

The Ireland to which Patrick was sent was a country of Celtic culture but of a very different Celtic culture from that which the Romanized Celts of Britain and Gaul had been used to for several hundred years. Ever since the Celtic race or races had first entered Ireland several hundred years before Christ the Irish had experienced no intrusion of an alien culture or external power. Neither the Romans nor the Picts had found it expedient to invade Ireland. In consequence Ireland offered a number of sharp differences in its life and behavior from the other countries of Western Europe. There were no towns. The nearest thing to a town in Ireland was a fortified place, perhaps a *rath*, as they are now known, or a prehistoric fort or a place of natural strength where the cattle and women and children of the tribe could be collected in a time of danger, when a neighboring tribe was raiding. Within this there might be some stone buildings, but not many. A local king would live in a permanent wood dwelling, but his subjects would not. Defences would be mostly of wood. Outside the fort the small, frail houses of wattle and turf would be very vulnerable to the enemy's attack but could easily be repaired when the enemy departed. The main occupation of the tribe would be cattle-breeding but of course some crops would be grown as well.

The basis of society was the tribe, a kind of extended family in which each member felt himself related by blood to the others. Each tribe would have a king, and some tribes would band together either under *force majeure* or through ancestral custom to form a larger group with a more important king. Patrick mentions both kings and subkings. One useful and common way of securing alliances between tribes was for the sons of the kings and nobles to be fostered by those of other tribes, to grow up under their protection. There was however no central authority at all and war or sporadic hostilities were endemic in Irish society. Society in ancient Ireland was carefully stratified into classes—kings, noblemen, craftsmen and *brehons*, freedmen and slaves—and a stranger such as Patrick would be at a grave disadvantage because the social system made no allowance for something as exotic as Christian clergy; they would be outcasts, analogous to the untouchables of Indian society, unable to call with confidence upon the protection of the law.

Irish law itself was not a written one, because there was no writing at all in ancient Ireland. It was however a real force in Irish society, preserved by special officials, whom Patrick calls judges (*Conf*. 53), whose task and lifelong occupation it was to know the vast corpus of oral tradition, embracing legend and cult and religion and law and custom, handed down from father to son; and it was by this that Irish society was regulated. Patrick refers to the custom of giving compensation for killing or injury (*Conf*. 53) which was one its of best features in that it must have prevented the occurrence of blood feuds. And though Irish society was illiterate it was not devoid of art or culture. The art of making beautiful objects in metal—gold or silver or bronze—had already been carried to a great height. The Celt's flair for color and the intertwined line was already expressing itself in patterns on clothes, in decoration on weapons and domestic ware, and in carving on stone. And included in the traditional lore of the Irish were legends and myths of a depth and beauty which could rival those of ancient Greece, tales of Queen Maeve and Deirdre and Cuchulainn and many others which delight us today as much as do those of Helen and Agamemnon and Achilles and Odysseus.

There must also have been groups and colonies of people of British race and culture living in Ireland. It was to these, Christians, to whom Palladius and perhaps at first Patrick were sent. Patrick refers to them at least once in his *Confession* (42). Pre-Christian Irish religion is difficult to reconstruct. The Celtic gods, until the Celts came in contact with the Romans, did not have special areas of experience attached to them, like Mars as a god of war, Diana of hunting, and they had a curious practice of appearing in double or triple forms (e.g., a two-headed god, or a group of three goddesses), and quite often had particular animals (a horse, a boar, a stag) associated with them. There must have been, as we shall see, some sort of cult of the sun in pagan Ireland in Patrick's day, though no identifiable sun god. There are traces of a fertility cult especially in connection with the inauguration of kings, and plenty of belief in magic.

Scholars in the past have made strenuous efforts to connect Patrick's career with events in the history of Ireland, with Niall of the Nine Hostages, with King Loeghaire and his headquarters at Tara, with the driving out of the Eoghanacht dynasty from their center at Navan Fort just outside Armagh by the Ui Neill dynasty who were destined to remain in one form or another a powerful force in Irish history for centuries to come. But all such efforts depend upon the assumption that the dates attributed to these persons and events by the Irish *Annals* are reliable, and this is an assumption which we cannot make. Archaeology has recently established, for instance, that Navan Fort was stormed and sacked at a period long before Patrick's day, about 200 B.C., and left for centuries untenanted thereafter.

Patrick tells us something of his career as a bishop in Ireland. His mission was in many ways successful. He converted, baptized, and brought to full membership of the Church thousands of people. He ordained many clergy in different places (though apparently no bishops). He encouraged the monastic life in some form at least. He experienced the very unpleasant shock caused by the massacre and enslavement of a group of newly-baptized Christians, the fruit of Patrick's work, by the soldiers of the British king Coroticus, and he reacted to this by writing the *Letter* which included a formal excommunication of Coroticus and his men. This *Letter* reveals that he was aware of opposition and resentment towards him and his work in the minds of many people whom we may confidently envisage as living in Britain. This opposition had manifested itself most strongly in the definite attempt which was made to impugn his character and probably also to deprive him of his office as bishop, an attack based on his confession of a sin many years before to his closest friend, and barbed by the betrayal of this confidence by that friend (see *Conf.* 26–32 and Commentary). Whether this attack was produced by his daring act, as an Irish bishop, of excommunicating a British king, we do not know, but the necessity of regarding the *Letter* as written not very long before the *Confession* tells slightly against this suggestion. The details of this are unclear, but though Patrick regarded it as a serious crisis in his career, he survived the attack and was apparently vindicated.

He traveled widely in Ireland, and claimed that he had evangelized in remote parts where no one had brought the gospel before. He met many vicissitudes and setbacks, including imprisonment. The sons of petty kings sometimes traveled around with him. His relations with the ruling authorities in Ireland cannot possibly have consisted of a series of spectacular triumphs, as the later Lives represent them. He tells us that he expects to be murdered or pillaged (*Conf.* 55,59). But he resolved that once he had set foot in Ireland as a bishop he would never leave its soil again, and he regards himself as on the side of, if not actually identified with, the Irish people (*Letter* 16).

Concerning where and how he died we know nothing at all. He may have lived in semiretirement at the end of his life, when he wrote the *Confession*. We can be quite sure that he did not die in Armagh, because if the monastery of Armagh could have made the slightest claim that it held his body or his relics it certainly would have done so, but it did not. The legend was that he was buried at Saul, a small village in Co. Down. But no cult of Patrick's relics or tomb grew up, which suggests that in fact when in the seventh century interest in Patrick began to grow and the potentiality of his name for purposes of propaganda (both ecclesiastical and political) began to be appreciated, nobody in fact knew where his body was. The burial-place of Patrick is covered with the darkness which falls like a curtain between the last words of his *Confession* and the next recorded mention of him in the year 632. This dark period witnessed a silent but luxurious growth of legend and folklore around his name, but also saw the preservation of his two written works.

III / St. Patrick's Character and Mind

Though Patrick's writings together make up only a small sum of literature they reveal to us Patrick's character more clearly than the much larger literary remains of other ancient Christian writers of

Latin reveal their authors' characters. The reason for this is that Patrick's writing is completely devoid of rhetoric. We may be grateful for the deficiency which he himself so much lamented. Even those writers who profess to bare their souls to us, even St. Augustine in his *Confessions*, cannot divest themselves of the rhetorical training which was part of their minds. They cannot but write for effect. This applies in fact to writers in other languages: do we really find the authentic Rousseau in his *Confessions*, for instance? But Patrick was incapable of writing for effect. It was all he could do to convey his thoughts to the reader without artifice, and even then he was not always able to do that. Patrick is, as very few people in the ancient world were, transparent to us, more transparent than Cicero was in his *Letters* or Ovid in his *Tristia*.

The root trait in Patrick's character is a sense of helplessness, of being vulnerable. As a boy of fifteen, the son of wealthy upper-class parents, perhaps spoiled, certainly waited on by servants, he had been mercilessly wrenched away from home by invading barbarians and carried as a slave into a land of foreigners whose language he did not know, whose culture he did not share, and had been forced to spend his days looking after sheep in all weathers. He was utterly alone. No attempts were apparently ever made to ransom the victims of Irish raiders, though Patrick later had clearly not abandoned hope of recovering their victims from British raiders and he knew of the system in operation whereby "Romans" in Gaul ransomed prisoners from the Franks. This appalling experience inflicted a trauma on Patrick's soul from which in a sense he never recovered. At the very end of his life, when he is an old man and a Christian bishop, he still refers to himself as a "poor ignorant orphan" (*Conf.* 35), as "an exile and refugee" (*Letter* 1), and as "poor and unsuccessful" (*Conf.* 55). He was always liable to regard himself as destitute of worldly help and pitiably vulnerable in the fell clutch of circumstance. This bent of his personality shows itself both in his extraordinary humility, indeed self-abasement, and in his curious pride that in spite of crushing misfortune he has made good in his evangelistic work in Ireland and that God had chosen him rather than some better educated person for this work, in his extreme sensitiveness to the realization that some people look down on him, and in his occasional moments of defiance of those who are better educated than he (e.g., *Conf.* 13).

But Patrick had another cause for the strong sense of inadequacy and inferiority which shows itself constantly in his writing: the deficiencies of his education. It was indeed the convention in his day for Christian writers to make certain protestations of inadequacy at the beginning of their works. Sulpicius Severus, in his *Life of St. Martin*, written at the end of the fourth century, for instance, does so. But it meant little more than the protesting of the parliamentary candidate that he has allowed his name to be put forward solely at the urging of his friends. In Patrick's case the protestations were made in deadly earnest. He uses the word "uncultivated" of himself twice (*Conf.* 1 and 12) and adapts rather pathetically a text in Ecclesiasticus which has nothing to do with the matter for the same purpose (*Conf.* 11, see Commentary). Three times he calls himself "very little educated," all in significant contexts, in the first and the second-to-last sentence of the *Confession*, and in the first sentence of the *Letter*. The last use of the term is particularly remarkable, because he is here beginning a letter of great severity in which he intends to excommunicate a British warlord and his soldiers, and in which one would have expected him to use all the authority at his disposal and reveal none of his weaknesses. But he cannot resist the pressure to admit his lack of education. He twice refers to his ignorance (*Conf.* 2 and 62), and three times to his unskilfulness (*Conf.* 10, 49, *Letter* 20).

> I had long had it in mind to write, but up to now I have hesitated. I was afraid lest I should *fall* under the judgement of men's *tongues* because I am not well read as others are. . . . For our speech and language has been translated into a foreign tongue, as can easily be demonstrated from the savor of my writing, the extent of my education and learning (*Conf.* 9). . . . But what use is a perfectly good excuse, particularly as I have the presumption to long in my old age for that which I did not achieve in my youth? . . . That is why I am now ashamed and am seriously afraid of revealing my unskilfulness, the fact that I cannot hold forth in speech to cultivated people in exact language (*Conf.* 10).

Patrick is no Mrs. Malaprop, confidently making dreadful solecisms while imagining that he is an elegant speaker. He makes malapropisms indeed, as anyone who has studied his Latin carefully can find out, but he suffers from the knowledge that he is liable to do so but cannot help himself.

Self-distrust does not necessarily engender humility. It can result, not only in a sense of inferiority but in an inferiority complex, when the sense of inferiority drives its possessor to noisy or violent self-assertion by way of compensation. But Patrick does not take that path. He has a genuine humility independent of his compulsive desire to disparage his own abilities and education. He is seriously anxious to attribute his success as an evangelist in Ireland to God and not to himself. He was a stone lying in deep mud when God chose to pick him out and elevate him (*Conf.* 12). He is doubtful whether he can respond adequately to God's calling to him (*Conf.* 13); he was not worthy of the destiny that God had prepared for him (*Conf.* 15). His close friend, the confidant of earlier years, had betrayed him basely at a critical period of his life, but the only reproach that Patrick makes to him is to regret that the friend was branded with God's disapproval in one of Patrick's visions (*Conf.* 32). Twice he reproaches himself for too great daring in boasting of God's goodness to him (*Conf.* 31 and 33). "Who am I, Lord," he says, "and what is my calling since you have worked with me with such divine power?" and he runs off into one of his long loosely connected sentences, clause following clause apparently at random in his desire to emphasize God's goodness to him (*Conf.* 34); and again, later, "But I see that I have been promoted beyond measure by the Lord *in this present age* and I was not worthy nor the kind of person to whom he might grant this" (*Conf.* 55). Thrice he expresses a positive desire for martyrdom (*Conf.* 37, 55, 59). His very last injunction expressed in the second-to-last sentence of the *Confession* (62) is a positive order that nobody should ascribe anything that God had done through him to Patrick's own credit.

Patrick was, however, capable of self-confidence and courage. Courage he showed preeminently in writing to Coroticus and his soldiers. Even as he writes he knows that by his act he will incur strong resentment and recrimination. One delegation with a letter has already been dismissed with scorn (*Letter* 3); he is the object of resentment (*Letter* 12) and dislike to Coroticus himself (6). But this does not prevent him from sending to Coroticus and his men a message which he himself calls "harsh and unpleasant" (*Letter* 1). They are heading towards Hell; he cannot any longer call them Christians nor "Romans" but outcasts. They must show signs of genuine and bitter repentance and try to make amends for their terrible crime. Until then they are placed outside the pale of the Church and no true Christian should have any social contact with them. Self-confidence had been engendered in Patrick by the success which his mission to Ireland had met: the thousands of converts, the candidates for the ministry, those who were ready to embrace an ascetic life in spite of setbacks and intimidation (*Conf.* 35–55). He can even be detected showing a certain pride in the conversion to an ascetic life of a beautiful Irish noblewoman (*Conf.* 37). Against the set of his mind and character, experience had in the end given Patrick self-confidence.

What supported in Patrick's character this combination of deep, almost pathological, self-abasement and self-confidence was his profound faith. His is not the faith which trusts that God will exempt its possessor from trouble and disaster. On the contrary, Patrick believes in God in spite of knowing perfectly well that God gives him no safe-conduct, and in spite of learning by experience that fellow Christians can show odious resentment that can at times express itself in violence and that the closest friend can shamefully betray. It is no coincidence that among all the books of the New Testament Patrick most frequently quotes the Epistle to the Romans. Patrick is assuredly no theologian. The controversies and heresies of the fifth century passed him by. But he has a good practical grasp of what justification by faith means. Early in his life he had experienced total disaster and utter misery; in his complete helplessness he had turned to God, and God had not failed him. The experience of finding in captivity and loneliness God's help when no human help was available profoundly affected his whole life. God had lifted him out of deep mud, had come to the rescue of his ignorance and blindness and had actually chosen him as his instrument for spreading the Gospel in Ireland. No vicissitude, not even the dreadful incident of Coroticus' massacre, could shake faith formed in those circumstances. "I have thrown myself into the hands of Almighty God who reigns everywhere," he says (*Conf.* 55). In the words of Kierkegaard, Patrick floats on seventy thousand fathoms of water and is not afraid.

With this faith goes gratitude to God. This is indeed the great motive for his writing the *Confession*. There are few chapters in that work where Patrick does not give thanks to God or express the desire to reward or pay him back for the benefits that he has given to Patrick. This gratitude has enabled him to overcome all the hesitations and obstacles standing between him and literary composition which did not come easily to him. The note of thanksgiving runs through the work like a refrain; indeed he exhausts his vocabulary in expressing the same thought again in different words. It is this quality of faith and of thanksgiving which imparts to Patrick's thought and doctrine the "evangelical" note which has often been remarked on. In a quite unfactional and undenominational way, indeed in an entirely Catholic way, Patrick was an evangelical person.

Patrick must have written other letters, though only one has survived. Perhaps the fact that it has survived, that it was thought to be worth preserving, copying and recopying, is a sign that it attained its object. The *Letter to Coroticus* is not like other episcopal letters of rebuke. It is too personal for that, too much like a cry of pain. What strikes home most deeply to Patrick is that his own authority as a Christian bishop has been contemptuously ignored. "They think it derogatory that we are Irish," he says (*Letter* 16). But in spite of his extraordinary Latin he manages to convey his feelings with remarkable accuracy. Patrick's syntax is often all astray, but his capacity to convey his feelings directly is all the greater because he cannot express them in elegant phrases. There is indeed a directness and honesty about his writing which to anyone who is well-read in Patristic Latin is most unusual.

His reason for writing the *Letter to Coroticus* is clear enough, but it is not so easy to determine his motive for writing his *Confession*. The comparison between Patrick's *Confession* and the *Confessions* of Augustine has often been made, and we cannot completely exclude the possibility that Patrick had Augustine's work in the back of his mind when he wrote his own. But, quite apart from the enormous difference of background and character between the two men, there are other differences worth considering between the two works. Augustine wrote his *Confessions* in the middle of his career, at the point when he knew that he had become decisively and permanently a Christian. It was not a complete autobiography, but it did follow roughly the successive main events in Augustine's life up to a point not very long before the time of writing, or at least up to his return to Africa after his conversion. Patrick's work was a survey of his whole life, made at the end of it, but a survey which confined itself narrowly to one particular aspect of that life: God's goodness towards the subject of the work. Apart from Scriptural names, names of only four individuals occur in Patrick's book, those of Patrick himself, of his father and grandfather, and of a man seen in a dream. He does not tell us (at least he probably does not tell us) the name of his close friend who betrayed him, of the beautiful Irish noblewoman who devoted herself to an ascetic life, of his master when he was a slave, of the captain of the ship which brought him back to Britain after his escape, of any of his clergy in Ireland. He breaks off the narrative of his life tantalizingly when we would like him to continue. He does not always keep to strict chronological order. He does not even in his *Confession* mention the episode with Coroticus. He does not mention the name of a single Irish king or subking.

The reason is that none of these things are necessary for his purpose. He is not writing his biography, nor even his spiritual biography. It is not a work like Bunyan's *Pilgrim's Progress* nor like C. S. Lewis's *Surprised by Joy*. It is an acknowledgment, a repayment (*retributio, Conf.* 3, 11, 12, 57) for all that God has done for Patrick and at the same time a description of the benefits which God has poured upon him. It necessarily tells us much about Patrick's life, but only so much as is necessitated by the theme, scarcely a word more. It corresponds pretty well to two of the senses of Augustine's *Confessions*, a confession of thanks and a profession of faith. But it is not in any serious sense a confession of sin. Patrick consistently states that God has at once punished his sin and reformed him in allowing him to be captured by Irish pirates (*Conf.* 1, 10). There is no echo in his *Confession* of the agonized sense of sin committed and forgiven which runs through Augustine's *Confessions*. Neither does Patrick indulge in the philosophical and theological questionings and speculations to be found in Augustine's work. At the same time, there is a certain wholeness and completed design in Patrick's *Confession* which prevent it from being a mere desultory stringing together of unconnected remarks. It is not difficult to divide it into the five sections indicated in the text. This division brings out the coherence and balance of the book.

But still we must ask, why did Patrick write it? He could not have expected a large circulation among an educated and interested audience, as Augustine certainly did. It must have given him considerable trouble to write in view of his difficulty in writing Latin. And there is a certain formality and finality about it. He includes a "Rule of Faith" (*Conf.* 4); he ends with the words "And this is my confession before I die." He wanted to put on record God's goodness to him in as public a manner as possible, of course. But he also wanted to vindicate himself finally against his detractors in Britain who must still have been fairly active. He tells us that he had spent a long time thinking about the work (*Conf.* 9). It was to be a kind of last will and testimony of his evangelistic work in Ireland; in fact, as he says, "so as to leave after my death a legacy to my brothers and my children whom I have baptized in the Lord, so many thousands of people" (*Conf.* 14). He knew when he wrote it that there were enough Christians of his making in Ireland to revere his memory and to preserve his record of God's goodness to him.

When we turn from the narrower consideration of Patrick's character to examine the contents of his mind, we are on more debatable ground. Many conjectures have been made about works which may have influenced Patrick and movements of thought which may be detected in his writings. We have already referred to the possibility of his having at some time read St. Augustine's *Confessions*. Others have suggested an influence of St. Cyprian, the bishop of Carthage who was martyred in 258 under the Emperor Valerian. In one passage (*Letter* 3) he may be echoing a sentence or so in Cyprian's work on the Lord's Prayer. And he has the same order (*Letter* 18) of "apostles, prophets and martyrs" as Cyprian has in one of his works and as occurs in the well-known Canticle *Te Deum* which was probably composed about 400.

But these are only isolated coincidences. We know nothing about the literature with which the British Church supplied its clergy. It may well have given them some snippets of quotations from the Latin theologians of the past, and the order of "apostles, prophets and martyrs" which seems to us unchronological may well have been a conventional one deriving from before Cyprian's time. The fact that the *Shepherd* of Hermas (mid-second century) speaks of stones being lifted up to make part of a tower, not the top of it, is not a convincing parallel with Patrick's picture of himself as a stone lifted out of deep mud and placed on top of the wall (*Conf.* 12). Efforts to support the argument that Patrick was influenced either by Pelagianism or anti-Pelagianism do not seem to me to have been successful.

We can be sure, however, of identifying one source in Patrick apart from the Bible. His "Rule of Faith" in *Confession* chapter 4 is certainly not of his own composition. The words "as the formula runs" (Latin *ut dicimus*), which is the best attested reading, suggests that Patrick is quoting one of the formulae of his British Church. The vocabulary and syntax of the "Rule" are not like Patrick's elsewhere, and it has been shown that the words in it follow a number of prose rhythms or patterns which were usually observed by writers of good Latin but are found almost nowhere else in Patrick's works. We can in fact identify one source, even though not perhaps a direct source, of this formula. It reproduces—in so many expressions that the reproduction cannot be coincidence—a "Rule" given by a writer called Victorinus, bishop and martyr, who uses the same word (*mensura*) for "Rule" as does Patrick (for details see the Commentary). It is possible that Patrick had read the work on the Revelation of St. John by Victorinus in which Victorinus set out his "Rule of Faith," but it is much more likely that Patrick is here reproducing the "Rule of Faith" of the British Church, especially as his "Rule" does not correspond exactly either to that of Victorinus nor to the "Rule" in the revised edition of Victorinus' work which Jerome brought out in 406.

A "Rule of Faith" was not precisely a creed; it was a short statement of the main articles, or some of the main articles, of the faith based on a creed in its structure but fuller and more variable than any creed, designed, as no baptismal creed was before the fourth century at least, to state and to test orthodoxy. The fact that Patrick's "Rule" includes one phrase (not found in Victorinus) apparently derived from a formula quoted by an Arian bishop of Milan in the middle of the fourth century is not surprising. It does not mean that the British Church nor Patrick himself had inclinations towards the Arian heresy, but only that the bishop of Milan was quoting a traditional Milanese creed and claiming that his doctrine was in substance the same as that of the Church of Milan. But this "Rule of Faith" quoted by Patrick has a peculiar interest and importance precisely because it is highly probable that it represents the "Rule of Faith" that Patrick was taught in the British Church, perhaps when he was being trained for ordination. It also suggests strongly that the British Church adopted the "Rule" of this martyr-bishop Victorinus whose works were widely read in the fourth century, that it received some more material from Milan, perhaps through the Church of Gaul, and that during the fourth century it also added several clauses designed to demonstrate and preserve the Church's orthodoxy among the controversies of that time.

Apart from the Bible, we cannot with confidence identify any other source in Patrick's works. Had he received his ecclesiastical formation in Gaul it is highly likely that he would have been more widely read. But it is significant that not only do we have no literature emanating from the British Church in the fourth century, but that nobody in the ancient world apparently knew of any. Even in the fifth century, when a few British theologians do appear, they seem to have received their theological education on the Continent and not in their native land. The ancient British Church always remained to some extent an ecclesiastical backwater where little intellectual life could be expected to flourish. Patrick reflects this state of affairs. It is however significant that among the ingredients in Patrick's Latin there can be detected not only the use of Vulgar Latin but also some liturgical and ecclesiastical terms and ideas. His ecclesiastical education was indeed not derived from a very bright center of culture and intellectual stimulus, but he certainly did receive a conventional ecclesiastical education.

The main source of Patrick's thought and teaching on matters religious was however the Latin Bible. This was not the Latin Bible which dominated the Middle Ages in the West, Jerome's translation, called the Vulgate. Jerome began this translation in the year 382, and though it was destined eventually to become the official Bible of the Latin-speaking Church, the Vulgate, like all new versions, took some considerable time to establish itself as the dominant translation. Christians are always slow to take up new translations, as they are to adopt new forms of prayer. For a long time Christians in the West distrusted this new-fangled Bible which did not include the favorite words and accustomed rhythms of the past, and Jerome was accused unjustly of all the sins of which in our day the compilers of the Revised Standard Version and the New English Bible and the many other contemporary translations have been thought guilty by conservative Christians. It is therefore not surprising that there is no clear indication that Patrick knew or used Jerome's Vulgate. But he certainly knew the Latin Bible used by the British Church supremely well. He constantly quotes the Bible, in season and out of season. Its phrases seem to have impregnated his mind and dominated his thought. Its words were household words to him. A serious and careful study of Patrick's use of Scripture has yet to be made, but a number of points about it should be noted here.

In the first place, his biblical interpretation is remarkably sound and sensible. When one has read the far-fetched allegorizing, the determined identification in the pages of the Bible of a complex and uniform system of thought which exists in the writer's fantasy but not in the Bible, the learned nonsense and high-flown imaginary constructions which appear in the biblical interpretation of the leading theologians (both Eastern and Western) of the fourth and fifth centuries—of Hilary and Ambrose and Jerome, or Athanasius and Basil and the two Gregories, of Eusebius of Caesarea and Epiphanius and Didymus—one turns with relief to the straightforward and simple use which Patrick makes of the Bible. He has the virtues of his deficiency. He is not well educated enough, he has not enough learning to indulge in the sophisticated silliness of much Patristic hermeneutics. He goes straight to the heart of the biblical message, to the promises of God in the Old Testament, to the redemption brought by Christ in the New. God's self-giving and love, God's demand of holiness and faith, God's trustworthiness and providence, the presence of the Holy Spirit in the hearts of believers: these are his themes; he has no difficulty in finding these in the pages of the Bible, and does not look further. He hears in a dream the words, "He who gave his life for you, he it is who speaks in you" (*Conf.* 24); he finds the Spirit praying in him "With groans that cannot be uttered" (*Conf.* 25, compare 20). Christ is to him the center of his life, in whom alone he will take an oath (*Conf.* 18), his true sun (*Conf.* 20, 59, 60), his Savior, the Master to whom he is a slave (*Letter* 10), his future Judge (*Conf.* 2, 4). In a particularly fine passage he says:

> I know for certain that poverty and disaster are more suitable
> for me than riches or luxury (but indeed the Lord Christ was
> poor for our sakes, but I am poor and unsuccessful and even
> though I were to desire riches I do not possess them) (*Conf.*
> 55).

Patrick has grasped the heart of the Gospel with remarkable
sureness.

His devotion to the Bible, however, is more than simply for purposes of doctrine and preaching. At times he seems to have an ap-
preciation of its power as almost magical. "That which I have set out
in Latin is not my words but the words of God and of his apostles and
prophets who of course have never lied" (*Letter* 20); he is probably
trying to impress, if not terrify, the more ignorant followers of Coroticus by quoting the Latin Bible at them, the sacred book written
in a solemn and to most of them incomprehensible language. At one
point in his *Letter* (2) he seems to be trying to create a solemn sound
to impress the ignorant British warriors by the use of Latin gerun-
dives (*condidi verba ista danda et tradenda militibus mittenda*). At
times he appears to present his argument by the tactic of a sea of
texts, overwhelming his reader with a barrage of biblical quotations
(*Conf.* 40, *Letter* 8). He almost bludgeons his readers with the Bible.

There are a number of curious misapplications of biblical passages
in Patrick's writings which suggest that he looks for Scriptural support or takes refuge in Scriptural language at any cost, in any circumstances, though in fact he never consciously employs the most widely
used Patristic hermeneutical device, that of allegory. At *Confession*
11 he quotes a version of Isaiah 32:4, "Stammering tongues will
swiftly learn to speak peace," to suggest that God will enable him to
compensate for his insufficient education. In *Confession* 37 he uses
a sentence from Ecclesiasticus 29:30 (23) which he gives as "to bear
the reproach of my pilgrimage," applying it to his endurance of vicissitude while evangelizing in Ireland. In order to make this text
seem relevant he has not only accepted in a loose form the inaccurate
Latin translation of the original Greek (which in fact meant, "Do not
get a name for living on hospitality" [NEB]), but has also omitted a
negative, thereby altering the whole sense of the passage. At *Letter*
12 I have translated the quotation from Ecclesiasticus 9:17 (12) as "It
will be even as displeasing as Hell," but this must frankly be re-

garded as a smoothing over of an untranslatable passage. Here Patrick has altered a passage which is almost meaningless in the Latin Bible (translating an already obscure Greek passage), to produce a sentence which is even more meaningless though it sounds at first hearing solemn and impressive; no doubt this is the effect he wished to make. The most striking example of his modifying of the Bible to suit his circumstances occurs at *Confession* 11 where Patrick has converted a text which originally meant "farm-work ordained by the Most High" (Ecclus. 7:16 [15]), to mean "countrified ways created by the Most High." His acute sense of being a backwoodsman has induced him to fasten on this text as a justification of his episcopal office in spite of his lack of education.

One other point about Patrick's treatment of the Bible is worth noting. He knows the Latin Bible far better than he knows any other book. In fact his education in the Latin Bible has supplied a considerable part of his vocabulary. There are occasions when he uses a biblical phrase or sentence because no other means of expressing himself comes to his mind. Twice he uses the expression "I saw in a vision of the night" (Dan. 7:13) because he finds this the simplest way of saying that he had a significant dream (*Conf.* 23, 29). He describes his conversion while in captivity in Ireland in almost wholly biblical language (*Conf.* 2). He speaks of his defective grasp of Latin as his "slowness of tongue" (Exod. 4:10) at *Confession* 11. He describes himself not only as "uncultivated, in exile, very little educated" (*Conf.* 12)—all his favorite epithets for himself—but adds "I do not know how to plan for the future," a quotation from Ecclesiastes 4:13 which is not only remote from its Hebrew original but can only loosely be applied to Patrick. It serves however as a general description of his plight. At *Confession* 21 he expresses his release from those who were imprisoning him in the words used at Genesis 37:22 of Reuben sparing Joseph's life; the plot to ruin Patrick is introduced by words applicable to the prophet Daniel (*Conf.* 27; Dan. 6:5); Patrick's plight in captivity is summed up in St. Paul's words of his own sufferings (*Conf.* 27; 2 Cor. 11:27), and so on. The Bible was in fact for Patrick a book which supplied not only his spiritual but also his literary needs.

One of the most interesting points to study about Patrick is his visions. Normally the subject of the visions of an early medieval saint would be tedious and predictable. Virtually all such saints have visions. They are complete, informative, stereotyped, and quite incredible. Angels punctiliously deliver elaborate and detailed messages or characters from the Old and New Testaments administer conventional approval or rebuke. In the case of Patrick we find no such circumstances. Patrick describes no less than eight visions or, as he calls them, Messages (*responsa*), at *Confession* 17 (two), 20, 21, 23, 24, 25, and 29, and they form an important part of the examples of God's goodness towards him which he narrates.

They all occur in dreams. Sometimes they consist of short pungent messages with no surrounding context or explanation, like "You have been right to fast because you will soon return to your country" (17), or "You will be with them for two months" (21). But he also relates more elaborate experiences involving things seen as well as things heard, like the decisive vision of Victoricus bringing letters from Ireland and the call from the people of the Wood of Voclut to return to them (23), or the obscure but reassuring sight of his own face dishonored and God's disapproval of this degradation (29).

All these divine Messages have about them a remarkable verisimilitude. They have a kind of surrealist inconsequentiality which convinces us that Patrick actually experienced them. In his vision at the rising of the sun while he was with his shipmates, *Helia* and *Helios* are confused in a manner which seems to come directly from Patrick's subconscious (20, see the Commentary); Victoricus arrives with countless letters but we do not hear of more than the heading of one of them and we are left in the dark as to who Victoricus is (23).

Even more remarkable is his description of actually experiencing the Holy Spirit praying in him (25): "And another time I saw him praying in me and I was as it were within my body and I heard above me, that is above my inner man, and there he was praying earnestly with groans." It is directly reminiscent of the Eastern Orthodox tradition of the Spirit praying in the heart of the Christian, what is called "the prayer of the heart." There is nothing artificial, there are no conventional hagiographical stage properties about Patrick's descriptions of his spiritual experiences. They are remarkably convincing and impressive. It is clear that he was a man of deep and simple spirituality. Whether we are to call him a mystic is a matter of nomenclature and is unimportant. But obviously his prayer life was of prime importance to him ever since as a helpless captive he turned to God and would sometimes pray as many as a hundred times a day and earned from the wondering pagan Irish of the district the sobriquet of "the Holy Boy" (*Conf.* 16, 23). We may here have discovered the secret of his success as an evangelist, his integrity. He was a holy man, without self-seeking, with no ulterior motives beyond the desire to spread the Gospel. He also remained an attractive and entirely human person. This is an unusual combination of attributes.

The last point with which we must occupy ourselves in this survey of Patrick's character and mind is to investigate whether Patrick was a monk. Ever since Martin of Tours (who died in 397), it had been possible for a bishop to be a monk. It is possible that Ninian, who was certainly a bishop, was also a monk, and that Riochatus, who was certainly a monk, was also a bishop (see above p. 11). But when we say "monk" we must be careful not to read too much into the word. To us "monk" means a member of a specific community inhabiting a monastery and sharing a common life of prayer and perhaps some other service with fellow monks. And we mean the same of women when we call them nuns. But even in the fifth century monasticism as developed as this was rare in the Western Church. There were communities of that sort in parts of Gaul; we know of one in Lérins, another in Grincy in the Juras, another founded by John Cassian at Marseilles, and probably another established by Germanus at Auxerre. But they were all of recent growth, and we have no firm evidence of the existence of any such in Britain before the sixth century.

On the other hand, such monks and nuns as these were not the only type of monastic persons to be found in the Western Church. There were at least two other distinct forms of this kind of life. There was the individual ascetic who had chosen for himself a life of peculiar strictness involving celibacy, a meager diet, and a regime of prayer which he practised on his own either in his own house among others or in some deliberately chosen remote spot. This was how the prototype of all monks, Anthony of Egypt, had lived, and this was how Martin had started his career. By the fifth century there were many of these, either living in remote places like islands or mountain country or following such an ascetic way of life in their own houses. These might be called eremetical ascetics. But there was also a middle way, less widely known but undoubtedly practiced, between eremetical monasticism and the full-blown coenobitic, or communal, monasticism. This was what might be called familial monasticism. By this arrangement a man might follow a course of ascetic practice while in the company of others who would not be so bound. For instance, a bishop would have living with him in the episcopal house, probably next to or even connected with his cathedral, a number of people to form his staff, his assistants in running his diocese. They would all be living together but only one or two of them would follow an ascetic life. This seems to have been the case with the household of Patiens of *Lugdunum* (Lyons) in the middle of the fifth century. St. Augustine of Hippo seems to have followed such a regime among his staff at *Hippo Regius* in North Africa, and that strange and unworldly saint of the Balkans in the turbulent fifth century, Severinus, seems at one time to have been an ascetic member of such a "family."

Patrick certainly knew about and valued monasticism. Four times he mentions women who live lives of chosen and consecrated virginity (*Conf.* 41, 42, 49, *Letter* 12) and twice he mentions monks (*Letter* 12, *Conf.* 41), all of them encouraged and instituted by himself. In one passage he mentions other forms of ascetic life (see Commentary on *Conf.* 42), and it is quite clear that the "virgins" mentioned in *Confession* 42 are not living a coenobitic life but are individuals practising asceticism in their own homes which are sometimes hostile to their practice, and that this asceticism was adopted by all classes from noble to slave. There can be little doubt that Patrick had met all these forms of ascetic life in Britain, though he must have learned something more about them during his visit to Gaul (see Commentary on *Conf.* 43).

The question of whether Patrick was himself dedicated to an ascetic life is worth raising, even though it cannot be answered with any certainty. At one point (*Conf.* 44) he says, "I have not led the life of perfection as other believers have led it," which suggests that he was not an ascetic. But this is not a conclusive passage, because it could mean no more than that he has not led as strictly ascetic a life as some, though he has kept to some ascetic regime. In the same chapter he speaks of "the purity of sincere religion" which he has accepted for Christ. He also uses of himself more than once the expression "to imitate," meaning to live a life of imitation of Christ (*Conf.* 34, 59), and this is the term he uses to describe the behavior of those women who have chosen a life of religious virginity (*Conf.* 42), and in another place he urges his readers, "I would like you to follow the way of imitation and do more" (*Conf.* 47). These are by no means irresistible arguments, but they create in the mind of anyone who has studied Patrick's works carefully a certain impression that he had in Britain been living a life of asceticism in some form, if only because it is not like Patrick to urge his flock to do something which he is not ready to do himself. If one is to make a conjecture (and it is pure conjecture) it would be possible to envisage him as having lived in a condition of what I have called familial monasticism, perhaps on the staff of some British bishop.

Finally, something must be said about the significance of St. Patrick for today, and for any age. Surprisingly little interest has been shown in Patrick by English readers, though he undoubtedly was a native of the country that after his day was to be called England. Perhaps an American public may find him more interesting. Serious students of the history of the ancient Church, whether professionals or members of the reading public at large, have probably been put off by the legendary nonsense and hagiographical distortion which have presented him to later ages as a figure at once implausible and tedious. Uncritical eulogy and the well-intentioned embroidery of folklore tend in many cases to defeat their own ends.

First of all, Patrick was British. He might be described as an Ancient Briton. He is certainly the first and might even be described as the only British person before the conquest of a large part of the country by the Anglo-Saxons whose character and personality we can know and appreciate. We have some works of Pelagius and of Faustus of Riez who were born in Britain, but they are not such as to throw much light on their characters, and they display minds cultivated outside their native land. We have one long work and a few fragments by Gildas, a Briton of the sixth century, and they do indeed tell us something of him; but Gildas used a highly, indeed excessively, rhetorical style which largely serves to conceal from us the real man, and Gildas never wrote anything as revealing of himself as Patrick's *Confession* was of him. Otherwise we know very little more of any Ancient Britons, pagan or Christian, than their names. But Patrick was a Briton brought up under the Roman administration of the Britains, one who appreciated Roman civilization and Roman education and regarded those who had missed these things, such as the Irish and the Picts, as barbarians and outsiders, and who virtually identified Christianity with Roman culture and civilization. He is therefore a rarity among the figures of the ancient world; he is in this respect almost unique.

Next, Patrick is a Christian Briton. He is a representative of the ancient British Church, of that Christianity which existed in the British Isles before Augustine of Canterbury and before the monks of Iona. Very little has hitherto been known of this British Church and very little interest has been shown in it, though chance finds and archaeological investigation are bringing in more information about it almost every year. Because until recently almost all serious students of Patrick were dazzled by the spurious attractions offered by the later tradition about him, the light which he could throw upon the British Church was neglected. As long as he was thought to be a product of Auxerre or Lérins or Rome or even Tours, he was regarded as no more than a figure of minor historical interest. But when it is realized that he was in every sense the product of the British Church, he becomes an important source of information on a subject about which there is little evidence. He assures us of the existence in Britain of monastic life, if not coenobitic, at least in those earlier forms which we have already surveyed. A really thorough and careful examination of Patrick's biblical text would throw light on that unexplored subject, the biblical text of the British Church. We now know something of the value attached to confirmation in the British Church from Patrick's references to it. We know a good deal about the doctrine and biblical interpretation of that Church, if we may take Patrick as a representative figure. We know that British clergy apparently did not concern themselves greatly with allegorization or far-reaching speculation, but appear to have concentrated in an admirable way on what we today would call the heart of the Gospel.

Above all, we have in our hands, if we will take notice of it, the "Rule of Faith" of the British Church, for it is improbable in the extreme that the fourth chapter of the *Confession* is a purely personal statement of Patrick, if only because it is not framed in language characteristic of him. We know that this Church originally borrowed its "Rule of Faith" from bishop Victorinus early in the fourth century but that it enlarged this summary during the fourth century to admit clauses designed to exclude Arianism, and that part of this formula at least had found its way from Milan to Britain. Finally, we know that British Christians valued their bishops, because Patrick, though he is obsessively self-deprecatory, maintains stoutly the divine authority of bishops. If at the end of surveying the evidence supplied by Patrick we come to the conclusion that the British Church was very like the Western Church elsewhere, in Gaul or Spain, except a little more backward, a little less well equipped with intellectual resources, that is not very surprising.

Another point that makes Patrick significant is his Latin. This is a point that has scarcely yet been appreciated by the world of scholarship. One can take up books on Vulgar Latin syntax and grammar and find no mention of Patrick; one can read books of selected extracts from works written in Vulgar Latin and find passages from Etheria and from Gregory of Tours and many others but not a word from Patrick. And yet Patrick is an early and particularly interesting source of Vulgar Latin because his Latin represents the kind of Latin that was spoken in Britain, for which otherwise we have nothing but a few sentences written on walls and a few words incised on sepulchral stones. Latin did not in Britain develop into a modern Romance language, as in Gaul it developed into French, in Spain into Spanish and Portuguese, and in Italy into Italian. But it certainly was spoken in Britain and it must have been the main source for Patrick's Latin. Not only do we meet in Patrick's works many of the grammatical, syntactical, and idiomatic phenomena found in Vulgar Latin elsewhere, but occasionally we can conjecture that Patrick enriches our knowledge of that type of Latin with a construction or even a word unknown elsewhere. Philologists should pay more attention to this interesting and (one might almost say) newly discovered source.

Another reason for calling the attention of as wide a public as possible to Patrick is that his *Confession* is in its way a masterpiece. A masterpiece of elegant Latinity or of piercing psychological self-analysis it certainly is not. It cannot stand comparison with St. Augustine's masterpiece, and it is unfair to Patrick to compare the two. But in spite of its awkward expressions, its stumbling sentences, its loose constructions, and in spite of the fact that at times Patrick simply cannot convey what he wants to say, when at the end of his life he wrote his *Confession* he achieved a masterpiece. The primary quality which endears it to the reader is its honesty. Not only was Patrick incapable of disguising his inner thoughts by rhetoric, but he was in himself a remarkably honest person. The rambling sentences, the disjointed constructions serve in the end to make transparent, not always his immediate meaning, but the basic quality of his soul. In this work Patrick intended to tell us of God's goodness to him and his response to God.

In this he succeeded admirably. There is a balance, a movement and a coherence about the book which only makes itself felt when the *Confession* has been read several times. After reading it we feel that we know Patrick intimately. Of how many other authors in the ancient world could this be said? We have a large collection of Cicero's letters. How much do we know of the real Cicero after we have read them? Something, but Cicero was almost always writing in order to commend himself and in some at least of his letters he had one eye on a reading public. We have a large literary legacy from Plato. Does a reading of it leave us with the conviction that we know Plato intimately? It would not be easy to answer that question with a confident affirmative. But when we have read Patrick's *Confession* we are sure that we know him. And at times Patrick manages to achieve an eloquence and an effect more moving than the carefully contrived periods of Cicero and the artifices of Ambrose's style. His defiance of the "skilled masters of rhetoric" (*Conf.* 13) is impressive and succeeds in making us want to take his side. His description of the dream in which the people of the Wood of Voclut called on him to return to Ireland (23) is written in a style which is almost childish, devoid of deliberate art, expressed in the simplest of paratactic constructions. But it is immensely effective. Patrick is like John Bunyan in that the simplicity of his style enhances the effect of his story, and in that Scriptural vocabulary enriches rather than mars his style. The very last entirely simple sentence of all could not have been better devised by a consummate literary artist: "And this is my Confession before I die."

Patrick makes us feel that we know him intimately, and he also makes us like him. Cicero was very anxious that his readers should like him, but it is doubtful whether he succeeded in this aim. Patrick does not try, but he succeeds in doing so all the same. This is the final reason why Patrick is worth studying. The Patrick of later legend is self-righteous, invariably well-informed, unfailingly successful, inhuman, not hesitating to inflict lethal miracles when he thinks them necessary, much concerned with guaranteeing privileges to churches and monasteries, and very ready to hand out celestial insurance policies in what seems to be a highly competitive market. The historical Patrick is utterly different: he is very human, distrustful of himself, full of a delightful humility, by no means successful in everything that he undertakes, a holy man, a man of integrity, no fool in his episcopal office, courageous when circumstances require courage, concerned about slaughtered and kidnapped converts, compassionate towards the struggling slave-girl Christians, full of an admirable faith.

He has his faults. He is too much obsessed with his own inadequacy. He perhaps even shows some snobbery over his "blessed Irishwoman, an aristocrat of noble race very beautiful and of full age" (*Conf.* 42). His virulent hatred of the Picts goes beyond proper bounds. But he is attractive, attractive as few figures in the ancient world are. It is a fact that scholars of all nations who have taken the trouble to study Patrick's works have found in him a curious fascination which is rarely to be found in other characters. Except when he thinks it necessary to give us a vast list of biblical quotations to emphasize his point, he is never boring. We follow with interest, sympathy, and pleasure his story from the helpless boy dragged ruthlessly away from his home and his parents to exile and slavery, through all the incidents of an adventurous life, until we leave him an old bishop by his own wish forever separated from his native land, devoted entirely to his task of converting the Irish in spite of opposition and misunderstanding. His life ends as far as we are concerned in total darkness lit only by the will-o'-the-wisp of later legend. But he has left behind an imperishable memorial, his *Confession*.

Translation of St. Patrick's Works

Prefatory Note to the Translation

All translators of Patrick have to choose between expressing what
Patrick appears to mean in his Latin prose and reproducing in English the obscurity, vagueness, and clumsiness of his expressions. To
choose the latter alternative would be to give something of the flavor
of his work but also to puzzle and even distract the reader. I have
therefore chosen the former policy, but even then there are several
places where the English syntax is almost as disjointed as the Latin
or where the chapter consists of a series of loosely connected sentences piling thought upon almost random thought without a full
stop. I have noted some of these in the Commentary.

I have refrained from consistently reproducing in my translation
of Patrick's quotations from the Bible any contemporary English
translation of it, because Patrick's biblical text corresponds to no text
which has appeared in an English translation. He was in fact reproducing (sometimes from memory) for the most part a Latin translation of the Greek of the New Testament and a Latin translation of a
Greek translation of the Hebrew (and occasionally the Aramaic) of
the Old Testament. His Bible therefore differed considerably in
some details from ours. I have sometimes put the letters VL in brackets after a Scriptural reference, meaning that this is a peculiar reading or translation of the version (known to scholars as *Vetus Latina*)
which Patrick was for the most part using, and in some of the references I have had to give alternative chapters or verses in brackets,
because the order of the material differs in some ancient versions
from the order which some Christians of today are accustomed to
seeing in their Bible.

The Latin text of which this is a translation is that printed in *Saint
Patrick: Confession et Lettre à Coroticus*, par Richard P.C. Hanson
avec la collaboration de Cécile Blanc (Paris, Éditions du Cerf, Séries
Sources Chrétiennes no. 249, 1978).

Translation of St. Patrick's Works

The Letter to Coroticus

1. I Patrick, a sinner, very badly educated, in Ireland, declare myself to be a bishop. I am quite certain that I have received from God *that which I am.* Consequently I live among barbarian tribes as an exile and refugee for the love of God; God himself is the witness that this is true. It is not that I was anxious to utter from my mouth anything in so harsh and unpleasant a manner. But I am compelled by *zeal for God,* and the truth of Christ has aroused me out of affection for my neighbors and children for whom I *have given up* country and kinsfolk and *my own life even to death.* If I am worthy, I exist to teach tribes for my God, even though I am despised in some quarters.

2. I have written and set down with my own hand these words to be solemnly given, carried, and sent to the soldiers of Coroticus. I do not say, to my fellow citizens, nor to the citizens of the Christian Romans, but to the fellow citizens of devils, because of their wicked behavior. They live in death in an atmosphere of enmity, associates of the Irish and the Picts and of outlaws. Bloodthirsty, steeped in

1. 1 Cor. 15:10; 1 Macc. 2:54; Phil. 2:30.

58

Commentary on St. Patrick's Works

The Letter to Coroticus

1. It was the convention in the fifth century for ecclesiastical writers to express a sense of sinfulness and incapacity at the beginning of their works, but, as we shall see, Patrick's sense of insufficiency goes far beyond convention. Here he emphasizes strongly, in spite of his feeling of inadequacy, that he has full authority from God as an authentic bishop. We need not rush to the conclusion that he is a self-ordained or self-authorized bishop. There were very few, if any, of these in the ancient world. But he is conscious that there were strong forces in Britain (where Coroticus lived) who derided his authority and belittled his work, as his words in this chapter "even though I am despised in some quarters" indicate.

He was not of course literally a "refugee," because he had come to Ireland voluntarily; but Patrick was almost obsessively aware of the helplessness of his position in Ireland, and we shall see many more signs of this.

The *Letter* is "harsh and unpleasant" because it in fact excommunicates those to whom it is primarily addressed.

The expression "country and kinsfolk" is an alliteration in Latin as it is in English and it is a favorite one with Patrick; he was to use it twice more at *Confession* 36 and 43.

2. Patrick's Latin here is deliberately solemn-sounding, almost menacing: this is only one of the signs in this *Letter* that Patrick uses Latin as a sacred language which will impress its hearers, most of whom would not understand it, by its resonance.

Patrick indicates that he would have liked to call Coroticus and his men "fellow citizens" and "Romans" and "Christians," the first because they had inherited a tradition of civilization from the Roman Empire, the second because they were the heirs of Roman order and blood, the blood of innocent Christians, whom I have begotten in large numbers for God and have confirmed in Christ!

3. The day after the newly-baptized, still bearing the chrism, still in their white dress [had been killed]—it was giving out its scent on their foreheads while they were being ruthlessly massacred and slaughtered by the men who have been mentioned—I sent a letter by a holy presbyter whom I had taught from his childhood up, along

culture and even language, in contrast to barbarians and outsiders like the Irish and the Picts and the Franks, the third because they certainly were nominal Christians (otherwise, of course, excommunication would have been futile). But because of their outrageous behavior they have forfeited a right to any of these names. "Romans" was a word specially used for citizens of the former Western Roman Empire who either survived in independent enclaves among the invading barbarians or who, though under barbarian rule, retained their own culture, language, and system of law.

"Irish" translates a word which is literally "Scots." But then this is the word used generally throughout Europe for the Irish until at least the ninth century (cf. "John Scotus Erigena"). It was only many centuries after the Irish of northeast Ireland began to emigrate to southwest Scotland and settle and finally establish a regular kingdom that Britain north of the Solway and the Tweed began to be called Scotland. Patrick has another name for the Irish, *Hiberionaci*, and as far as we can see he uses either term indiscriminately.

The Picts were a race or perhaps a nation consisting of several races who had been known to the Romans (who gave them this name, meaning "the painted people," probably because they tatooed themselves) for several centuries. They later lived in the north of what is now Scotland, and especially the northeast, but in Patrick's day it is likely that they inhabited also some more southerly parts of Scotland, Fifeshire and perhaps parts of Galloway. If Coroticus was king in Dumbarton on the Clyde he would have been in a good position to do business with them. They spoke their own language, some traces of which have come down to us in writing, but nobody has yet been able to decipher it. Patrick calls them literally "apostates" (outlaws in this translation), but it does not seem likely that this implies that they had been Christians and had apostasized; it is more likely that this is just a general word of abuse. It is not known why Patrick shows such peculiar animus against them.

3. In the fifth century, at least among peoples newly evangelized, Christian initiation took the form of a single comprehensive ceremony including baptism, during which the candidates stood naked in a tank or pool while water was poured copiously over them, then a ceremony for which they put on new white clothes and in which

with clergy, asking that they would kindly spare us something from the booty or from the prisoners whom they had taken. They laughed at them.

4. That is why I do not know what I am to grieve for more bitterly, whether those whom they captured who were killed or those whom the devil has deeply ensnared. They shall inherit Hell equally with him in eternal punishment, because of course, *he who commits sin is a slave* and is called a *son of the devil*.

5. Therefore let every man who fears God know that they are estranged from me and from Christ my God, *on whose behalf I am fulfilling a mission*, murderers of fathers and of brothers, *greedy wolves devouring the people of the Lord as they would eat bread* (as in the text *The wicked have destroyed your law, O Lord*) which in the last times he had well and carefully planted, and it was established by the favor of God.

6. I am not exceeding my rights. I have a part with those *whom he called and predestined* to proclaim the Gospel among no inconsiderable persecutions *even to the end of the earth*, even though the en-

4. John 8:34,44. 5. Eph. 6:20; Acts 20:29; Ps. 14(13):4; Ps. 119(118):126. 6. Rom. 8:30; Acts 13:47; Matt. 16:19.

the bishop laid his hands on them and anointed them with chrism or sweet-smelling ointment, and then the Mass or eucharist at which they communicated, in both kinds, for the first time. The second stage was what Patrick calls confirmation but he certainly means it also to include the third stage of communion. The newly-initiated would wear their white clothes for several days afterwards and would as far as possible preserve the chrism on their foreheads. Patrick's statement that he had educated the presbyter whom he dispatched "from his childhood up" shows that he must have been in Ireland for a long time when he wrote this *Letter* because we have no reason to assume that he would have educated people thus while he was in Britain. This implies that he must have written the *Letter* quite late in his career as a bishop in Ireland, and prohibits us (as do several other points) from postulating a long interval between the writing of this *Letter* and the composition of the *Confession*.

5. This is Patrick's first reference to "the last times," but by no means his last. He regarded himself as commissioned by God to evangelize the last people in Europe, those who inhabited the shores of the extreme West, beyond which there was nothing but barren sea, and saw this as corresponding to the final stage of history, after which, all nations having been evangelized, the world and history would end. It is possible that we can detect in this conviction some ripple of the enormous psychological and political disturbance caused by the capture of Rome by Alaric and his barbarian Gothic army in 410.

6. Patrick might have been thought to have exceeded his rights in excommunicating Coroticus and his men, who were not resident in his diocese and indeed lived in a different country, Britain, not Ireland. But he replies to this hypothetical accusation that bishops are given authority by God to rule his Church as they think fit. In spite

emy grudges me this by means of the despotic rule of Coroticus who does not fear God nor his bishops whom he chose and granted to them supreme, divine, lofty power, that *those whom they bound on earth are bound in heaven also.*

7. And that is why, *you holy and humble in heart,* you must not dance attendance on people like these, *nor take food* nor drink with them nor must their alms be accepted until they have rigorously made satisfaction to God bathed in tears, and have freed the slaves of God and baptized maidservants of Christ, for whom he died and was crucified.

8. *The Most High rejects the gifts of the wicked. He who offers a sacrifice from the property of the poor is like him who slaughters in sacrifice a son in the sight of his father. The riches,* it says, *which he has dishonestly gathered will be vomited out from his stomach, the angel of death drags him, he will be savaged by the wrath of dragons, the tongue of the serpent will kill him and unquenchable fire devours him.* And so, *woe to those who fill themselves with that which is not theirs,* and *what does it profit a man that he should gain the whole world and suffer the loss of his own soul?*

9. It is too long to set out or mention every text, to choose proof texts through the whole Sacred Law about greed of this sort. Avarice is a deadly sin. *You are not to covet your neighbor's property. You are not to commit murder.* A murderer cannot be with Christ. *He*

6. Matt. 18:18   7. Dan. 3:87 (Song of the Three Holy Children, 65); 1 Cor. 5:11.   8. Ecclus. 34:23–24(19–20); Job 20:15–16,26; Hab. 2:6; Matt. 16:26.   9. Exod. 20:13,17; 1 John 3:15,14.

of his sense of personal insufficiency Patrick insisted upon the authority of his order.

The "despotic rule" of Coroticus is a phrase translating a term in Latin which probably echoes the title taken by the rulers of the successor kingdoms into which Britain broke up after the end of Roman rule—*tyrannus* (tyrant). In Latin it meant someone who ruled illegally or irregularly, but it may have become almost a technical term by now; it may even have looked and sounded like a British word meaning "lord of territory," and if this were so it would assist in the process of making the term one in common use.

The word for "bishops" here is literally "priests," but then in Patrick's day the bishops, and not the presbyters, were the priests *par excellence*.

7. This is the point in the *Letter* where Patrick formally excommunicates Coroticus and his men. The chapter is addressed to all Christians who may meet these delinquents. The disciplinary system of the Church, which was well established in Patrick's day, would not readmit these sinners to communion until they had performed long and severe penance.

8. This is one of those places where Patrick, as it were, flings the Latin Bible at the head of his opponents. This string of quotations is almost an incantation.

who hates his brother is reckoned a murderer, and *He who does not love his brother remains in death*. More guilty is he who has defiled his hands with the blood of the children of God whom he has recently gathered at the ends of the earth through my exhortation, poor though I am!

10. It cannot be thought that I came to Ireland without God or on purely secular business! Who compelled me? I was *bound in the Spirit* so as never to revisit any of my kinspeople. Surely it was not my doing, this holy compassion which I have been exercising towards that nation which once took me captive and dealt havoc among the men and women servants of my father's house? I was a free man in worldly position; my father was a decurion. Indeed I bargained away my aristocratic status—I am neither ashamed nor sorry—for the benefit of others. In short I am a slave in Christ to an outlandish nation because of the unspeakable glory of *eternal life which is in Christ Jesus our Lord*.

11. And if my own people do not recognize me, *a prophet has no honor in his own country*. Perhaps we are not *from the same sheepfold* and do not have *the same God as Father*? So it says, *He who is not with me is against me and he who does not gather with me scatters*. It is not good enough. *One destroys, another builds up*. *I do not seek my own interest*. It is not to my credit, but it is God *who put this concern into my heart* so that I should be one of the *hunters or fishers* whom God long ago predicted beforehand [as appearing] *in the last days*.

10. Acts 20:22; Rom. 6:23.   11. John 4:44; John 10:16; Eph. 4:6; Matt. 12:30; Ecclus. 34:28(23); 1 Cor. 13:5; 2 Cor. 8:16; Jer. 16:16; Acts 2:17.

10. Here Patrick returns to the contempt in which he is held in Britain, manifested most keenly in the fact that Coroticus had dared to carry out this massacre, and he justifies himself against it. He incidentally tells us quite a lot about himself; he had been kidnapped years before by the Irish and had returned good for evil by revisiting Ireland in later life as a preacher of the gospel.

"The men and women servants of my father's house" serves to suggest, with several other pieces of evidence, that Patrick's father was a wealthy landowner. Patrick can claim that he bargained away his status because, arriving as a stranger in the much stratified society of ancient Ireland, he had no place in the social scale, no status, like an outcast in India, and therefore was not protected by law or custom. He was the prey of any who attacked him. In Britain he had not only been a free man protected by both British and Roman law but a member of the upper class. The statement that his father was a *decurion* means that Calpornius, his father, belonged to the higher class of native Romanized Britons whose privilege—as well as irksome duty—it was to collect taxes for the Roman government. We shall hear more about this later (see on *Conf.* 1).

11. Patrick here makes it crystal clear that Coroticus and his men were British and were nominally Christians. It hurts him keenly that he should have been humiliated by those who were of his own nation and his own religion.

"Hunters and fishers"; Patrick returns to this theme in *Confession* 40.

12. I am the object of resentment. What am I to do, Lord? I am greatly despised. Here are your sheep savaged and made a prey, and by the gangsters already mentioned, at the behest of Coroticus with evil intent. One who betrays Christians into the hands of Irish and Picts is far from the love of God. *Voracious wolves* have swallowed up the flock of the Lord which was increasing in Ireland nicely as a result of hard work, and the sons of the Irish and the daughters of subkings [were] monks and virgins of Christ—I cannot count them. This is why *good men being hurt should not please you, it will be even as displeasing as Hell.*

13. What Christian will not shrink from making merry or enjoying a good meal with people of that sort? They have filled their houses with the loot of dead Christians, they are living on the spoil. In their wretched state they do not realize that they are offering deadly food to their friends and their children, just as Eve did not understand that in fact she was handing death to her husband. So are all who do evil. They are bringing on themselves death as eternal punishment.

14. This is a custom among the Roman Gauls who are Christians: they send suitable Christian men to the Franks and the other nations with so many thousand *solidi* to ransom baptized people who have been captured. You, on the contrary, murder them and sell them to an outlandish race which does not know God. You are virtually handing over the *members of Christ* to a brothel. What hope in God have you, or who can approve of you or hold any polite conversation with you? God will judge. For it is written, *Not only those who do evil, but also those who consent to it are to be damned.*

12. Acts 20:29; Ecclus. 9:17(12).   14. 1 Cor. 6:15; Rom. 1:32.

12. Patrick here suggests that Coroticus' raid was a deliberate act of defiance aimed at him. We seem to sense too a faint suggestion that behind Coroticus or with him stand other opponents of Patrick in the British Church, people whose hostile activity will be referred to more openly in the *Confession*.

His reference to children of royal families in Ireland embracing an ascetic life will be amply substantiated in the *Confession*. Irish society at that time was as full of kings, lesser or greater, as Tsarist Russia was of princes. Patrick however never makes reference to a High King, and it is most unlikely that any such person existed in his lifetime.

"It will be even as displeasing as Hell" is a desperate attempt to make sense of a quotation from Ecclesiasticus which after being translated from the Greek into the Latin of Patrick's Bible made almost no sense at all and has been further reduced to meaninglessness by Patrick's pulling it right out of its context and misunderstanding the syntax. No translator of Patrick into any language has been able to make sense of it.

14. Patrick's reference here to the practice of the Christians in Gaul is particularly interesting because it suggests that he had visited that country; and we shall find support for this at *Confession* 32 and 43. We know anyway from Patrick's own case that apparently no machinery existed for ransoming prisoners taken by the Irish. Once again "Romans" here means people of Roman culture and language (and Patrick appears to regard them as virtually identical with Christians) living either among or next to barbarians who had recently come into the country by way of invasion.

The *solidus* was a gold coin, 72 of which went to the pound, first minted by the Emperor Constantine the Great (c. 270–337) but

15. I do not know *what I can say* nor *what I can speak* concerning those of the children of God who are dead whom the sword has so outrageously sorely smitten. It is indeed written *Weep with those who are weeping* and in another text, *If one member grieves all members should grieve with it.* Consequently the church *mourns and laments her sons* and her daughters whom the sword up to now has not yet killed, but they are exiled and deported into distant countries, where sin prevails openly, terribly, shamelessly, that is where freeborn people are sold, Christians are brought into slavery, and especially among the lowest, vilest outlaws, the Picts.

16. Therefore I will exclaim with sorrow and grief: O most beautiful and most beloved brothers and children *whom I have begotten in Christ* [whose numbers] I cannot count, what am I to do for you? I am not capable of assisting God or men. *The wickedness of the wicked has prevailed over us. We have been treated* like *outsiders.* Perhaps they do not believe that we have received *the same baptism* and have *the same God as Father.* They think it derogatory that we are Irish. As the text says, *Do you not have one God? Why has each one deserted his neighbor?*

---

15. John 12:49; Rom. 12:15; 1 Cor. 12:26; Jer. 31:15.   16. 1 Cor. 4:15; Ps. 65(64):3(4); Ps. 69(68):8(9); Eph. 4:5,6; Mal. 2:10.

widespread during the last century of the Western Roman Empire and much copied by barbarian rulers on the Continent after the collapse of that Empire, but not minted in Britain nor imported in any large quantities after the year 410. Patrick clearly thought that maintaining machinery for ransoming was a sign of civilization in the society that used it.

Patrick's reference to "a brothel" reflects his anxiety for the fate of the female captives. It is clear from a number of scattered pieces of evidence that the sexual mores of ancient Irish paganism were very different from those of Christianity and it seems likely that this legacy from paganism continued to affect early Christian Ireland for some time.

15. His reference to the open prevalence of sin among the captors of his converts probably arises from the same fear.

16. This pasage is addressed to all those whom he has converted and baptized during his ministry in Ireland, not specifically to the victims of Coroticus. Once again he deplores the failure of Coroticus and his men to recognize and honor the Christianity which they and their victims have in common.

His statement that "they think it derogatory that we are Irish" is curious because Patrick was of course not Irish but British. In fact the translation is based on a text which has been emended from a reading which would mean "we are native-born Irish." This would be an even more startling statement in Patrick's mouth. We can imagine him identifying himself for the moment with his Irish converts, but we cannot imagine him describing himself as born in Ireland. This is not an early example of a national antagonism between the British and the Irish. Nationalism, whether British or Irish, was

17. Consequently I mourn for you, I mourn, my dearest. But again I rejoice within myself; I have not *labored* in vain nor has my pilgrimage been *useless*. And if this crime, so horrible, so unutterable, had to happen, thanks be to God you baptized believers have departed from this world to Paradise. I observe you; you are beginning the journey to where *there will be no night nor mourning nor death any more, but you will rejoice like calves loosed from their tethers and you will tread down the wicked and they will be as ash under your feet*.

18. You therefore will reign with the apostles and prophets and martyrs. You will receive eternal kingdoms, as he himself witnesses in the text *They will come from the east and from the west and will sit down with Abraham and Isaac and Jacob in the kingdom of Heaven. Outside are dogs and poisoners and murderers;* and *As for the liars and perjurers, their part is in the lake of everlasting fire*. It is not for nothing that the apostle says, *Where the good man will scarcely be saved, where will the sinner and wicked lawbreaker find himself?*

19. Now this is why Coroticus and his gang of criminals, rebels against Christ—how will they feel, since they distribute baptized women as prizes for the sake of a wretched temporal kingdom which of course may disappear in a moment? *Like cloud or smoke which is dispersed by the wind, so will* deceitful *sinners perish from the face of the Lord. The good however will feast in great confidence* with Christ. *They shall judge nations and rule over* wicked kings for ever and ever. Amen.

17. Phil. 2:16; Rev. 22:5,21:4; Mal. 4:2–3(3:20–21).   18. Matt. 8:11; Rev. 22:15; Rev. 21:8; 1 Peter 4:18.   19. Wisd. 5:15(14); Ps. 68(67):2–3; Wisd. 5:1;3:8.

then far in the future. It is the sense of superiority of those who regarded themselves as inheriting the legacy of the Roman Empire over those whom they regarded as semicivilized outsiders.

17. Patrick now turns to address the souls of those who have been murdered by the minions of Coroticus. He believes that they are on their way to heaven, not exactly because they are martyrs but because they have been killed very shortly after baptism when their sins had been forgiven and they had scarcely had time or inclination to commit any further serious sin. This is not a doctrine of Purgatory, though it would not have been inappropriate nor impossible for Patrick, as a fifth-century bishop, to teach such a doctrine. The words "you have departed from this world to Paradise" occur again in a short list of sayings later attributed to Patrick and they are the only words in that list which are likely to be authentic.

19. The incoherence in the English translation reflects the incoherence in the original Latin.

20. *I bear witness before God and his angels* that it shall be just as he signified to me, unskilled though I am. That which I have set out in Latin is not my words but the words of God and of apostles and prophets, who of course have never lied. *He who believes shall be saved, but he who does not believe shall be damned.* God has spoken.

21. I earnestly request that whatever servant of God shall volunteer to carry this letter that it may be by no means shortened or added to by anybody, but on the contrary it may be read in the presence of all the tribes and when Coroticus himself is present. May God then guide them to reform their attitude to God at some point so that they should repent, even though it be late, of what they have so indecently done—murder committed on the brothers of the Lord—and release the baptized captive women whom they have previously taken, so that they may deserve to live to God and be made whole here and in eternity. Peace to the Father and to the Son and to the Holy Spirit. Amen.

20. 2 Tim. 4:1; 1 Tim. 5:21; Mark 16:15–16.

20. Here Patrick openly refers to the fact that his quotations are from the Latin Bible; he expects his audience to be overawed by the unintelligible words from the sacred, almost the magic, book. But even here Patrick cannot help referring to his lack of education.

21. Patrick appears to assume that his *Letter* will be read out several times to several different audiences, and probably that it will be translated also.

His reference to the captive women need not mean that the soldiers of Coroticus had massacred the men and captured the women; the captives and the victims were of both sexes. But the reference reflects Patrick's anxiety for the particular fate which, he suspected, awaited the women.

Finally, Patrick cannot invoke God's peace upon Coroticus and his men; he has just put them out of the peace of the Church; yet he wants to end his *Letter* in conventional style. So, awkwardly, he calls for peace *upon* and not *from* the three Persons of the Trinity.

Translation of St. Patrick's Works

The Confession

I / His Youth: His Capture by Irish Pirates; God's Goodness to Him

1. I am Patrick, a sinner, most uncultivated and least of all the faithful and most despised in the eyes of many. My father was Calpornius, a deacon, a son of Potitus, a presbyter, who was at the village of Bannavem Taberniae. He had an estate nearby and it was there that I was captured. At that time I was nearly sixteen years old. For I did not then know the true God and was carried away captive as had been so many thousands of people—it was according to what we deserved because *we had deserted God* and *we had* not *observed his commandments* and we had not been obedient to our bishops who used to warn us about our salvation. So God *brought upon us the anger of his indignation and scattered us among* many *nations,* even *to the end of the earth,* where now I am to be found, in all my inadequacy, among foreigners.

---

1. Isa. 59:13; Gen. 26:5; Isa. 42:25; Jer. 9:16; Acts 13:47.

Commentary on St. Patrick's Works

The Confession

I. 1. Once again Patrick's self-depreciation goes well beyond the conventional, and he here repeats his conviction that he has enemies and those who despise him. We should probably place them in Britain and, as the sequel will show, include in them more than simply Coroticus and his men.

We should not be surprised that both Patrick's father and grandfather were clergy; clerical marriage was countenanced in one form or another well into the Middle Ages, indeed as late as the eleventh century, and in Patrick's day carried no particular stigma with it. What should surprise us is that Calpornius was both a deacon and an owner of an estate; see the Introduction, pp. 22–23. It is likely that Calpornius was attached to *Bannavem Taberniae* as a deacon, not as a *decurion*. Most villages (*vici*) would have been too small to achieve an *ordo* of *curiales*, that is a committee of upper-class administrative officers. We must frankly admit that we do not know where *Bannavem Taberniae* is nor even if that is the right form of the name of Patrick's birthplace. (See Introduction, p. 19). But his mention of an estate, and (*Letter* 10) of the many servants on his father's estate and this claim to noble birth assure us that Patrick came from the upper class of native British society and must have been brought up in wealth and comfort.

Patrick insists here and also at *Confession* 27 that his upbringing did not include any contact with a living faith in God, which probably reflects badly on Calpornius' motives in seeking deacon's orders. See Introduction, p. 23. The experience of being at an early and impressionable age wrenched ruthlessly away from a comfortable home and

2. And it was there that the Lord *opened the understanding of my unbelieving heart,* so that I should recall my sins even though it was late and *I should turn with all my heart to the Lord my God,* and *he took notice of my humble state* and pitied my youth and my ignorance and protected me before I knew him and before I had sense or could distinguish between good and bad and strengthened me and comforted me as a father comforts his son.

3. So that is why I cannot keep silent, *and it is not expedient,* about the great acts of goodness and the great grace which the Lord generously gave me *in the land of my captivity;* because this is my repayment, after I have been chastened and have recognized him *to praise and confess his wonderful works* among *every nation that is under the sky.*

4. Because:
there is no other God nor was there ever in the past nor will there be in the future except God the Father ingenerate, without beginning, from whom all beginning flows, who controls all things, as our formula runs: and his Son Jesus Christ whom we profess to have always existed with the Father, begotten spiritually before the origin of the world in an inexpressible way by the Father before all beginning, and through him were made things both visible and invisible; he was made man; when death had been overcome he was received into Heaven by the Father, and *he gave to him all power above every name of things heavenly and earthly and subterranean and that every tongue should confess to him that Jesus Christ is Lord and God;* and we believe in him and await his Advent which will happen soon, as *judge of the living and the dead, and he will deal with everybody according*

---

2. Luke 24:45; Heb. 3:12; Joel 2:12, 13; Luke 1:48.   3. 2 Cor. 12:1; 2 Chron. 6:37; Isa. 25:1(Ps. 88:6[89:5]); Acts 2:5.   4. Phil. 2:9–12; Acts 10:42; Rom. 2:6.

all his friends and relations to live as a slave among people whom he regarded as uncivilized foreigners inflicted upon Patrick's personality a trauma from which in one sense he never recovered. See Introduction, p. 36.

3. Here Patrick first mentions his main reason for writing the *Confession*. It was to thank God for what he had done for Patrick, and to put on record concrete examples of God's goodness to him. He counts the appalling experience of being captured by Irish pirates as the first example; he consistently interprets it as God's act at once punishing and reforming him. See *Confession* 12,28,33.

4. This is the only passage where we can be certain that Patrick is reproducing another document. This is a "Rule of Faith." In chapter 14 he calls it "The Rule of Faith of the Trinity." No doubt he was taught it when he was being trained for the ministry. It is a precious document because it is wholly likely that we have here the "Rule of Faith" of the ancient British Church. We can trace at least part of its pedigree. Its form and some of its wording are taken from a similar Rule of Faith included in a book on the Revelation of St. John the Divine by a writer called Victorinus who was bishop of a town called *Poetavio* (modern Pettau) in the Balkan peninsula at the end of the third and beginning of the fourth century. He was later martyred in the last great persecution of the Christian Church organized by the Emperor Diocletian, and this made his works very popular. Obviously they were read by Christians in Britain, who decided to model their Rule of Faith taught to clergy (and perhaps to laity too) on his. But there is more in Patrick's Rule of Faith than this. He mentions the Trinity; Victorinus does not, and several of his clauses referring to Christ's divine status show signs of having been added

to their deeds and *he poured out upon us richly the Holy Spirit* the gift and pledge of immortality, who makes those who believe and obey to be *sons of God* and *coheirs with Christ* and we confess and adore him, one God in the Trinity of sacred name.

5. For he himself said through the prophet, *Call upon me in the day of your trouble and I will deliver you and you will glorify me*, and elsewhere it says *Now it is honorable to display and confess the works of God.*

6. However though I am unsatisfactory in many points I want my brothers and relations to know what I am like, so that they can perceive the desire of my soul.

7. I am not ignorant of *the witness of my Lord* who testifies in the Psalm, *Thou shalt cause those who speak falsehood to perish.* And in another place it says *The mouth which tells lies kills the soul.* And the same Lord says in the gospel *The idle word which men shall have spoken they shall give an account for it in the Day of Judgment.*

8. So that is why I ought *with fear and trembling* seriously to dread this pronouncement in that day on which nobody will be able to absent himself nor escape, but *we shall* all certainly *render an ac-*

---

4. Titus 3:5–6; Rom. 8:16–17.   5. Ps. 49(50):15; Tob. 12:7.   7. 2 Tim. 1:8; Ps. 5:6; Wisd. 1:11; Matt. 12:36.   8. Eph. 6:5; Rom. 14:10,12; 2 Cor. 5:10.

as a result of the great Arian controversy, which raged during most of the fourth century, and which did not begin till several years after Victorinus' death. On the other hand, there are no signs in this Rule of Faith of clauses which owe their presence to any of the lively controversies which occupied the Church during the fifth century. We can be confident that this Rule of Faith is not Patrick's own composition. Its Latin style, markedly different from the rest of the *Confession*, alone should convince us of that. In this solemn final review of God's dealing with him during the whole of his career, he wishes to include at an early point a statement of his orthodoxy, and he does this very appropriately by reproducing the Rule of Faith of his native Church.

6. "Brothers" almost certainly means "fellow Christians," as it does elsewhere, see *Confession* 14, 47, 49, *Letter* 16, 21. His "relations" cannot mean his father and mother, who must by now be long dead, but the members of the extended family which was so important in any Celtic society, even a Romanized one, like British society.

count even for the smallest sins *before the judgment seat of the Lord Christ*.

9. Wherefore I have long had it in mind to write, but up to now I have hesitated; I was afraid lest I should *fall* under the judgment of men's *tongues*, because I am not well read as others are, who have successfully assimilated law and sacred literature, both disciplines equally, and they have never made a change in the languages which they have spoken from childhood, but rather have continually improved them to entire fluency. For our speech and language has been translated into a foreign tongue, as can easily be demonstrated from the savor of my writing, the extent of my education and learning, because, it says, *the wise man will be recognized by his speech, and so will his understanding and his knowledge and teaching of the truth*.

10. But what use is a perfectly good excuse, particularly as I have the presumption to long in my old age for that which I did not achieve in my youth? In fact my sins prevented me from grasping securely that which I had previously read carefully. But who believes me even though I may repeat what I have already stated? I was a youth, indeed almost a beardless boy, when I was carried away captive, before I could know what I should seek or what I ought to avoid. That is why I am now ashamed and am seriously afraid of revealing my unskilfulness, the fact that I cannot hold forth in speech to cultivated people in exact language, expressing what my spirit and mind desire and my heart's sentiment indicates.

11. But if I had had the same talent as the others had of course I would not have remained silent *for the sake of repayment* [of God], and if by chance it appears to some people that I am pushing myself forward with all my ignorance and *slowness of tongue*, still all the same it has been written: *Stammering tongues will swiftly learn to speak peace*. How much more should we who are, in the words of Scripture, *a letter of Christ for salvation to the end of the earth*,

9. Ecclus. 28:30(26); Ecclus. 4:29(24).   11. Ps. 118(119):112(VL); Exod. 4:10; Isa. 32:4; 2 Cor. 3:2–3, Acts 13:47.

9. Here Patrick begins to indicate the kind of people with whom he keenly feels himself to contrast unfavorably. It is important to note what it is that he declares them to possess and himself to lack, a knowledge of law, a sound grasp of Latin and (as he will presently add) a capacity for writing rhetorical speech. This is precisely what any Romanized British boy would have learned at the third stage of Roman education, in the school of the *rhetor*. For the important bearing of this on our determining the details of Patrick's life, see Introduction p. 21. He here admits openly that he finds Latin difficult to speak and write. His sense of inferiority caused by his consciousness of his deficiency in education haunted him all his life.

10. When he says that his sins prevented him from completing his education he does not mean that he was lazy and careless at school; on the contrary, he says that he had "read carefully." But his education was interrupted by his captivity in Ireland, and he always regards this as God's punishment for his sin. The final sentence of this chapter can only be translated by inspired guesswork because— as if to demonstrate finally his incapacity in Latin—his language is so vague and muddled that we cannot be sure of his exact meaning. It is particularly when he is trying to describe his own feelings that Patrick's grasp of Latin fails him.

11. Two striking but only distantly appropriate quotations from the Bible in this chapter illustrate the variety and wide-ranging nature of Patrick's use of Scripture. Isaiah 32:4 is from a passage describing the ideal Messianic kingdom which is to appear in the future when all human disabilities will be healed. Ecclesiasticus 7:15(16) is even more remote in its application; the passage really means "agricultural operations are created by God," and urges the reader not to despise them; Patrick takes it to mean "countrified ways are created by God," and not without a certain pathos invokes it to justify his lack of sophistication. Patrick was a man of one book—the Latin Bible—

attempt something written, if not learned still firm and strong, *written on your hearts not with ink but with the Spirit of the living God.* And in another place the Spirit testifies *and countrified ways created by the Most High.*

12. So it was that I, originally uncultivated, in exile, very little educated, and *I do not know how to plan for the future*—but this I do know certainly that *before I was humiliated* I was like a stone that lies in deep mud, and *he who is mighty* came and in his compassion raised me up and exalted me very high and placed me on the top of the wall; and consequently I am strictly bound to cry out so as to make some repayment to the Lord for those benefits of his which were so great here and in eternity which the mind of men cannot calculate.

13. So now, *you great and small who fear God*, be amazed and you, skilled masters of rhetoric, listen therefore and look. Who was it who roused me out from those who appear to be wise and *powerful in speech* and in every subject, yes inspired me, whom this world hates, more than the others to see if I was capable—and if only I could!—of serving faithfully with fear and reverence and without complaint that nation to which the love of Christ carried me, and he granted that, if I were to be worthy, I should at last do them good service during my lifetime with humility and sincerity.

14. Consequently I must teach from the *rule of faith* of the Trinity, without fear of danger to make known the gift of God and *eternal comfort*, to promulgate the name of God everywhere fearlessly and faithfully, so as to leave after my death a legacy to my brothers and my children whom I have baptized in the Lord, so many thousands of people.

15. I was not worthy nor the sort of person to whom the Lord should make this gift, should grant me so much grace after troubles and such great difficulties, after imprisonment, after so many years spent

11. 2 Cor. 3:2–3; Ecclus. 7:16(15).   12. Eccles. 4:13(VL); Ps. 118(119):67; Luke 1:49.   13. Rev. 19:5; Luke 24:19; Heb. 12:28.   14. Rom. 12:3; 2 Thess. 2:16.

and he was determined to use this book to the utmost—and sometimes beyond it!

12. This simile of the stone taken out of deep mud in order to be placed on the top of the wall does not come from the Bible; in the mouth of someone like Patrick, this is surprising, and it makes us realize that it comes from his heart or (to put it in another way) from the depth of his unconscious mind. Alongside his altogether unusual sense of insufficiency there existed in Patrick's mind a deep and touching trust in God.

13. Here again Patrick gives us valuable information about the people compared with whom he feels himself inferior. They are "skilled masters of rhetoric," and "wise and powerful in speech." It is wholly likely that they were British clergy who, Patrick knew, would be likely to despise him for his lack of education, and who may have formed part of the opposition to his work in Ireland which, as we shall see, became so strong as nearly to ruin his whole career. But here Patrick is triumphing over them, though he ascribes his survival and his achievement to God. His Latin in the middle of this chapter again begins to break down under the stress of emotion.

14. Here, as in other places (*Conf.* 50, 51, *Letter* 5), Patrick claims that his lifework had succeeded in establishing a numerous and flourishing Church in Ireland. We have no reason to doubt his word here.

among that nation, a thing which I never at any time in my youth hoped or expected.

II / His Escape from Ireland to Britain

16. But when I had come by ill luck to Ireland—well every day I used to look after sheep and I used to pray often during the day, the love of God and fear of him increased more and more [in me] and my faith began to grow and my spirit to be stirred up, so that in one day [I would say] as many as a hundred prayers and nearly as many at night, even when I was staying out in the woods or on the mountain, and I used to rise before dawn for prayer, in snow and frost and rain, and I used to feel no ill effect and there was no slackness in me (as I now realize, it was because the Spirit was glowing in me).

17. And it was there that one night I heard a voice saying to me in a dream, "You have been right to fast because you will soon return to your country," and next after a little time I heard a Message saying to me, "Look, your ship is ready"—and it was nowhere near but lay perhaps two hundred miles away and I had never been there before nor did I have any acquaintance among the people there—and at last after a while I took to flight and deserted the man with whom I had been for six years and I came in the power of God who was guiding my way for a good purpose and I had no fear all the time until I reached the ship.

18. And on the day that I reached it the ship had moved out from its berth and I talked to them in order to secure the means of sailing

II. 16–22. Patrick now proceeds to tell us something of how he succeeded in escaping from Ireland after his capture. But because this is not an autobiography but a record of God's goodness to him he omits much and takes much for granted which we would like to have explicitly described.

16. "Woods and mountains" give us no clue to the place of his captivity, because almost any part of the coast of Ireland exhibits those features, or did so in Patrick's day.

17. The first two Messages from God recorded by Patrick; and like all the others, they occurred in dreams. The Latin word here translated "Message" (*responsum*) occurs five more times (*Conf*. 21, 29, 32, 35, 42) and is almost a technical term in Patrick for a divine communication made (usually in a dream) to Patrick or somebody else.

"Your country" makes it perfectly clear that the destination at the end of Patrick's journey was Britain, and not, as some scholars obsessed by the later tradition about Patrick have conjectured, Gaul.

"Two hundred miles" is incompatible with Patrick's place of captivity being anywhere on or near the east coast of Ireland because he could not possibly have needed to travel nearly two hundred miles in order to reach a ship for Britain had his place of captivity been there; this therefore rules out his traditional place of captivity, Mount Slemish in Co. Antrim in the northeast of the island.

18. The ship had either been brought down from the beach and set afloat or brought alongside a pier. It may have been a construction

with them and this annoyed the captain and he answered me sharply
in anger, "No way! You are not to try to travel with us!" and when I
had heard these words I walked away from them to go to the hut
where I was staying, and as I went I began to pray and before I could
finish my prayer I heard one of them and he was shouting loudly
after me, "Come back quickly, because these people are calling
you," and I returned to them at once, and what they said to me was,
"Come on, because we are taking you on trust; make an alliance with
us by whatever way suits you." On the same occasion I had refused
to suck their nipples out of fear of God but I on the contrary had
expected from them a journey on condition of swearing my fidelity
by Jesus Christ, and at this I gained my point with them and we set
sail straight away.

19. And after three days we made landfall and we traveled for
twenty-eight days through uninhabited country and their food ran
out and *famine prevailed over them,* and one day the captain turned
to me and said, "What now, Christian? You say that your God is
great and almighty; why then can you not pray for us? Because we
are in danger of starvation. For we have a problem about meeting
any human being." I then confidently said to them, *"Turn* in faith
with all your heart to the Lord my God, because nothing is impossible to him, [asking] that he may today send food across your way
until you are full because he has abundant resources everywhere,"
and with the help of God that is what happened: the next thing was
a herd of pigs appeared on our route in front of our eyes, and they
killed many of them and they stayed there two nights and were well
refreshed and their strength was renewed, for many of them had
collapsed and had been *left half-dead* by the wayside, and after that
they gave the fullest thanks to God and I was esteemed in their eyes
and from that day onwards we had abundant food. They even found
wild honey and *offered a bit to me* and one of them said, "It is a
sacrificial offering." I thank God that from that moment I ate no more
of it.

19. Gen. 12:10; Joel 2:12–13; Luke 10:30; Luke 24:42.

of wood and hide, the direct descendant of which is the modern
curragh used in the west of Ireland; quite large examples of this type
of craft were used. There has been considerable debate as to the
identity of Patrick's shipmates. It had long been assumed that they
were traders, and the reference to dogs which we shall consider later
(see below p. 91) encouraged this notion. But the more recent suggestion that they were not traders but raiders is more plausible. This
would explain their determination to extract from Patrick an oath of
fidelity. They did not want him to betray them as soon as they
reached Britain. Patrick apparently made no great objection to their
marauding activities, but refused to take an oath in the pagan way.
Sucking the nipples is paralleled as the ancient Irish pre-Christian
way of sealing a bond of friendship. We shall find several other examples later of Patrick's objection to pagan customs.

19. Because of Patrick's description of their journey through desert
country, the suggestion was made by the well-known historian of the
ancient world, J.B. Bury, in his *Life of St. Patrick*, that Patrick and
his companions were traveling not on British soil but in Gaul, since
a terrible invasion of Gaul by barbarian tribes from east of the Rhine
took place in 407, and it is known that they left a trail of devastation
and desolation behind them as they moved westwards over Gaul. If
this were so, it would date Patrick's return from captivity, and indeed his whole career, very neatly. But, ingenious though the conjecture is, it is not at all plausible. It is unlikely that the boat would
have made the journey from Ireland to Gaul in as short a time as
three days; it is unlikely that even hordes of barbarians would have
left Gaul in quite such a state of depopulation as Patrick depicts; it is
wholly unlikely that Patrick would expect us to realize that he was in
Gaul when he has virtually told us that he was going to Britain (see
above, p. 87). And we can account for his story quite easily by
assuming that the party found themselves in a part of Britain which
was covered by dense forest, as much of Britain was in Patrick's day,
and as it remained well into the Middle Ages. They did not travel in
a straight line but probably wandered around in circles. This theory
is slightly supported by Patrick's reference to "wild honey" which
literally translated means "honey of the woodland" (*mel silvestre*).

20. But that same night I was sleeping and Satan tempted me strongly, which I shall remember *as long as I shall be in this body*, and there fell on me something like a huge stone, and none of my limbs capable of moving. But how was it that it occurred to me, ignorant in spirit that I was, to call on Elijah? And while this was taking place I saw the sun rising in the sky and while I was crying out "Elijah! Elijah!" with all my strength, the next thing that happened was that the radiance of that sun fell upon me and at once dispersed from me all paralysis, and I believe that I was succored by Christ my Lord and his Spirit was at that moment crying out on my behalf, and I hope that so it shall be in the *day of my tribulation*, just as it says in the gospel, *"In that day,"* the Lord testifies, *"it will not be you who will speak but the Spirit of your Father who speaks in you."*

20. 2 Peter 1:13; Ps. 49(50):15; Matt. 10:19–20.

The pigs were either wild pigs or domestic pigs which had escaped and turned wild.

The expression "their strength was renewed" is the translation of a reading in some of the manuscripts (*carnes*). Others, the greater number, read a word which means "dogs" (*canes*). Many scholars in the past have accepted the better attested reading and imagined that Patrick's companions were traders in, among other things, Irish wolfhounds, which were indeed prized in the ancient world as hunting dogs, and have surmised that Patrick (who had been handling sheep for six years) would be good at handling dogs. But this theory is most improbable: the ancients did not have the same feeling for animals as we do today; Patrick would have been unlikely to mention the sad fate of dogs; if the party had been accompanied by dogs it is likely that they would have eaten them in the last stages of starvation. Patrick's contribution to the expedition was probably his knowledge of the British language, not his flair for dogs. We must abandon the touching picture of Irish sailors feeding their dumb chums on pork chops.

Patrick austerely refuses the honey because it has been offered to or associated with a pagan god.

20. It is hardly possible to appreciate the point of this account of a confused experience narrated by Patrick unless we realize that the Latin for Elijah is *Helias* (vocative *Helia*) and that the Greek for the sun is *helios*. Patrick assuredly was no Greek scholar, but that much he did know. In his subconscious mind by this resemblance of words the prophet Elijah (who was regarded as a kind of Old Testament Christian saint in the ancient Church) and the rising sun became associated or identified. We shall hear of Christ as the sun in chapters 59 and 60.

21. And I next underwent captivity again many years afterwards. So I remained with them the first night. But I heard the divine Message saying to me, "You will be with them for two months." And that is what happened; on the sixtieth night *the Lord delivered me from their hands.*

22. Even while we were traveling he provided for us food and fine and dry weather until on the tenth day we reached human habitations. As I have said already, for twenty-eight days we made our way through uninhabited country and on the night that we reached human habitations we actually had nothing.

III / Other Manifestations of God's Care

23. And next a few years later I was in Britain among my parents who [had] received me for their son and earnestly requested me that I should now after all the troubles which I had experienced never leave them, and it was there that *I saw in a vision of the night* a man coming apparently from Ireland whose name was Victoricus, with an uncountable number of letters, and he gave me one of them and I read the heading of the letter which ran, "The Cry of the Irish," and while I was reading aloud the heading of the letter I was imagining that at that very moment I heard the voice of those who were by the Wood of Voclut which is near the Western Sea, and this is what they cried, *as with one voice,* "Holy boy, we are asking you to come and walk among us again," and *I was struck deeply to the heart* and I was not able to read any further and at that I woke up. God be thanked that after several years the Lord granted to them according to their cry.

---

21. Gen. 37:21.   23. Dan. 7:13; Dan. 3:51 (VL) (Song of Three Holy Children 28); Acts 2:37.

21. Patrick here makes one of his disconcerting chronological leaps, reminding us that this is not a formal autobiography. His liberation from dream-induced paralysis reminds him of an incident which occurred much later, when he was a bishop in Ireland. He refers to it briefly and then in the next chapter reverts to the narrative of his return from captivity in Ireland.

III.23. Patrick tells us nothing of what happened between the incident which he has just related and this vivid account of a significant dream. But there is no reason to think that he had visited Gaul in between, nor that he is here describing his return to Britain after the continental tour which later tradition attributed to him.

About Victoricus we know nothing, except that names ending with *-icus* are often regarded as of Celtic origin. Conjecture has, as usual, been busy here, and has tried to identify him with a certain bishop Victricius of Rouen who is known to have visited Britain some time in the last decade of the fourth century; but there is no sure ground for this identification. Victoricus is clearly the origin of the guardian angel Victor who looks after Patrick in an obliging way in the later stories about him.

Almost all reading (and, one suspects, praying) was done aloud in the ancient world, even by people who were quite alone.

It is impossible to avoid the conclusion that the "Wood of Voclut which is by the Western Sea" was situated by the Atlantic on the west coast of Ireland. Patrick was in Ireland when he wrote these words; the only sea to the west of him was the Atlantic. To imagine that he could mean the Irish Sea between Britain and Ireland is absurd. It is equally farfetched to think that "the children of the Wood of Voclut" were not the people among whom Patrick had spent

24. And on another night—*I do not know, God knows* whether it was in me or beside me—[someone was speaking] in the most elegant language which I listened to but could not understand, except that at the end of the speech he spoke these words, "*He who gave his life for you*, he it is who speaks in you," and at that I woke up full of joy.

25. And another time I saw him praying in me and I was as it were within my body and I heard above me, that is above my *inner man*, and there he was praying earnestly with groans, and while this was going on I was in amazement and I was wondering and I was considering who it could be who was praying in me but at the end of the prayer he spoke to the effect that it was the Spirit, and at that I woke and I recalled that the Apostle had said, *The Spirit assists the weaknesses of our prayer: for we do not know what it is right for us to ask for; but the Spirit himself intercedes for us with groans that cannot be uttered, which cannot be expressed in words*; and in another place, *The Lord our Advocate intercedes for us*.

24. 2 Cor. 12:2,3,   25. Eph. 3:16; Rom. 8:26. 1 John 2:1.

the years of his captivity, especially as in the dream they call on him
to come and live among them "again." This means that the place
where he was kept a slave for six years was on the west coast of
Ireland, and the necessity which faced him when he escaped of traveling two hundred miles fits in well with this. When therefore Tirechán tells us that the Wood of Voclut was in the district of Tirawley
(near the modern small town of Killala, on the sea-coast of Co. Mayo
not far from the border between Co. Mayo and Co. Sligo), we can
well believe him. Tirechán himself came from that area, and place
names survive unchanged much longer than any other form of tradition. These conclusions are, of course, fatal to the later story that
Patrick spent his captivity on Mount Slemish in Co. Antrim.

24. Once again Patrick's Latin becomes incoherent, unless we are
to suspect a very early corruption in the text now beyond emendation.

26–33. Patrick now begins to write about an episode in his life which
was obviously very important but which, to our loss, he treats in so
allusive and obscure a way that it is difficult to reconstruct it at all
and impossible to be sure of all the details. It is fairly sure that this
event or series of events happened when Patrick had been a bishop
in Ireland for some considerable time, whether before or after the

26. And when I was attacked by some of my seniors who came and [brought up] my sins against my onerous work as bishop *I was violently pushed to make me fall*, both here and in eternity; but the Lord kindly spared his stranger and sojourner for the sake of his name and greatly supported me when I was downtrodden. How amazing that I did not come to a bad end in failure and disgrace! I pray God that *it may not be reckoned a sin to them*.

26. Ps. 117(118):13; Deut. 24:15(?2 Tim.4:16).

massacre of his converts by Coroticus' men and the *Letter* which it evoked we do not know. The incident consisted of an attack on Patrick, a grave accusation made against him, an attempt, in all probability, to ruin his career and perhaps to have him deposed from the episcopate. We can be certain that this assault came from Britain and not from Ireland or Gaul, if only because one of the main agents in it was his close friend, who certainly was in Britain. Anyway, as it is perfectly clear that Patrick assumes consistently that his mission arose from Britain and that he was responsible to the British Church, so the likelihood of this threat originating in Britain is very great. Beyond these broad conclusions, we have to piece together the story as best we can from unexplained allusions and ambiguous expressions. We must always remember that Patrick was professing to give a list of God's acts of goodness towards him, not to give a coherent, orderly account of his own career.

26. Who these "seniors" were is far from clear. The word could mean the older monks in a monastery; but Patrick, whatever his previous career may have been, was not at this point writing from a monastery. It could mean simply "older men." But on the whole it is likely to mean senior bishops in positions of authority in the British Church. If so, then it is likely that this accusation must be placed some considerable time before Patrick was writing and probably therefore well before he wrote his *Letter to Coroticus*. The evidence in that *Letter* that Patrick still has enemies and detractors in the British Church could be a reflection of the aftermath of this accusation and its further ramifications.

That Patrick says that these seniors came to him suggests a deputation sent from the British Church (or a part of it) across to Ireland. But his Latin here is very obscure. The expression "my onerous work as a bishop" can on any reasonable interpretation only imply that the accusation was made and the deputation sent some time after Patrick had gone to Ireland as a bishop, and must rule out the theory (which some have held) that this accusation was made before Patrick went as a bishop to Ireland, while the question of his mission was being canvassed and considered.

"How amazing . . . . failure and disgrace" translates a particularly difficult (because colloquial) piece of Latin. It could be translated in

27. *They found a charge against me* after thirty years, a word which I said in confession before I was a deacon. Because of my scruples I related to my dearest friend out of a contrite heart what I had done once in my boyhood, in fact in a single hour, because I did not yet have self-control. *I do not know, God knows*, if I was then as much as fifteen years old, and I was not a believer in the living God, and had not been since my infancy, but I lay in death and disbelief until I was punished, *and I really was humbled by hunger and nakedness*, and that daily.

28. No, I made the journey to Ireland against my will, to the point when I was near collapse, but this was rather for my good, because I was reformed by God through the experience, and he molded me so that I should today be what was once far from me, so that I should take trouble and labor for the salvation of others, whereas then I used to take no thought even for my own.

27. Dan. 6:5; 2 Cor. 12:2,3, Ps.118 (119):75; 2 Cor. 11:27.

a different sense, "I didn't half come to a bad end. . . ." But the context and the sequel make this unlikely; Patrick never admits that he was in the wrong in this matter.

27. Patrick's point here is that though he had committed the sin which was made the burden of the accusation against him, he had been punished for it by God and had made reparation for it by his sufferings during his captivity. We do not of course know what the sin was. That it was a sexual fault is pure conjecture, though not implausible conjecture. It was possible in the ancient Church to discipline clergy for sins committed before they were ordained. It is interesting to learn that before being ordained as deacon Patrick had confessed his sins to a close friend, one who was, we may be sure, older than he, and who was therefore very probably at the time of the accusation a "senior" and a bishop. Regular auricular confession before communicating at the eucharist had not yet in Patrick's day become either a custom or an obligation, but it was quite usual to have a kind of spiritual director whom you could consult about the state of your soul. It is interesting to note that the custom of regular auricular confession was to appear first about two hundred years after Patrick's day in the Irish Church. Some debate has been occasioned about whether the "thirty years" here referred to are to be reckoned from the commission of this sin or from the confession of it. If we take the first option, then this accusation came when Patrick was relatively young in his episcopal ministry, aged not yet forty-five. But it is better to take the second option and assume that the thirty years date from the moment of Patrick's confessing the sin; after all, he refers to "the word" which he confessed.

28. This chapter is simply a reinforcement of his point that he had already been punished and made satisfaction for the sin which was being used against him.

29. Therefore on that day in which I was rejected by the people already mentioned above, that night *I saw in a vision of the night* a dishonoring inscription placed against my face, and at the same time I heard the divine Message saying to me, "We have seen with displeasure the face of the man denounced here," revealing the name. And he did not declare, like this, "You have seen," but "We have seen," as if he would have taken his side, just like the text *"who touches you touches as it were the apple of my eye."*

30. That is why *I give thanks to him who supported me* in everything, that he did not prevent me from the enterprise which I had resolved on nor from my work which I had learned from Christ my Lord, but rather from that moment *did I feel* no slight *power in me* and my faith was approved in the sight of God and men.

29. Dan. 7:13; Zech. 2:8(12).   30. 1 Tim. 1:12; Luke 8:46.

29. This is a particularly obscure passage, not least because Patrick is describing a dream which he had and he manages to preserve in his description the surrealist inconsequentiality of dreams (see Introduction, p. 48). The best explanation is that Patrick saw in his dream his own face as if on a coin with an inscription round it and the inscription, instead of being a eulogistic one (as in coins of Roman Emperors), was derogatory of Patrick. This divine Message then expressed displeasure that these derogatory words should have been pronounced against Patrick, and declared that God, the author of the Message, was on Patrick's side. It is possible, however, to interpret the account in another way, and to take the Message as declaring, "We have seen with displeasure the face of the man in question" (literally "the designated man"), and in this case the man indicated would be Patrick's former close friend but now treacherous enemy (the Latin word used is *designatus*). It has even been suggested that Patrick here gives us the name of his friend and enemy—Designatus—which is not at all impossible as a name in the Late Roman Empire. There is, however, one serious objection to this interpretation, and this is that in chapter 43 Patrick uses the same word ("denounce" or "designate") again, and here it clearly means "denounce" or "convict." Further, Patrick has just referred to a face, and certainly that was his own face. It is not likely that he would now switch to referring to the face of his accuser. But as we are here dealing with such stuff as dreams are made of we must not be dogmatic in our conclusions.

30. The "enterprise" referred to here can be nothing but his going to Ireland as a bishop, and this would appear to support the view that this attack took place when Patrick was being suggested as bishop but had not yet been sent. But there are almost insuperable difficulties in this view, even if we discount the reference to his onerous episcopate (see above, p. 97). We must allow thirty years between Patrick's confessing the sin when he was about to be made deacon and the attack. It is unlikely that he was made deacon before the age of thirty, or at the earliest twenty-five; we must then allow a long period of time, at least twenty years but probably more, for Patrick's residence as a bishop in Ireland before he sends to the soldiers of Coroticus a presbyter whom he has brought up from child-

31. And so it is that *I declare boldly* my conscience does not reproach me either now nor for the future; I have it on God's testimony *that I have not lied* in the words which I have related to you.

32. On the other hand however I am sorry for my close friend because of our being thought worthy to hear such a Message as that. And I even entrusted my soul to him! And I learned from some of the brothers that before that occasion for defending myself (at a time when I was not present nor was I even in Britain nor was the matter initiated by me) he, even he, was canvassing for me. He even had said to me with his own mouth, "Listen! You are to be promoted to the rank of bishop," though I was not worthy. But what came over him later that he should have publicly vilified me of all people before everybody, good and bad, on the score of that which he had previously granted to me voluntarily and gladly, as also had the Lord, who is *greater than all?*

31. Acts 2:29; Gal. 1:20.   32. John 10:29.

hood (while he was a bishop in Ireland). If we attempt to place the accusation before he went to Ireland as a bishop we have to assume a lapse of the better part of fifty years, and perhaps more, between his being made deacon and his writing the *Letter*. This is in the last degree implausible. We must place the attack during his period as bishop in Ireland, and quite far on in it, and assume that Patrick refers to this "enterprise" and thanks God for calling him to it because had his accusers succeeded in their aim his whole mission and work would have been ruined, and Patrick is expressing gratitude that they were not. The approval of Patrick's faith by God and man probably refers to his eventual vindication against his accusers, by some official decision in the British Church, we may conjecture. The later story in the *Annals* and elsewhere that Patrick went to Rome and was confirmed in his see by Pope Leo I probably arose out of their statement but is historically worthless.

32. Once again Patrick gives us precious information about himself but once again his allusive manner of giving it makes it difficult for us to understand its exact bearing. It is clear that the activities of his friend on his behalf were exercised during the period when Patrick's name was being canvassed as one who might be sent from the British Church as a bishop to Ireland. That he says that this took place before he had occasion to defend himself against attack confirms the view that the attack came when Patrick had been for some time bishop in Ireland. It seems best to assume that Patrick is referring to the behaviour of his former friend on three quite separate occasions: (1) When Patrick was absent from Britain he supported Patrick's cause while the question of sending a bishop to Ireland was being discussed and considered. (2) When the decision to send Patrick had been made and Patrick was back in Britain again he announced the news to him that he had been chosen to go as a bishop to Ireland (and this supports the view that the former friend was himself a bishop). (3) At a later time, perhaps much later, when Patrick had already been a bishop in Ireland for some time, his former friend treacherously

33. I have said enough. And yet I ought not to hide the gift of God which he has lavished upon us *in the land of our captivity,* because I then sought him resolutely and there I found him and he preserved me from all forms of wickedness (so I believe) *because of his indwelling Spirit* who *has been active* in me up to this day. [I am speaking] *boldly* again. But God knows, if it had been a man who spoke this to me, perhaps I might have kept silence for the love of Christ.

34. And this is why therefore I give unwearying thanks to my God, who kept me faithful *in the day of* my *trial,* so that today I can offer to him confidently in sacrifice my life as a living victim to Christ my Lord, who *preserved me from all my difficulties* so that I can say as well, *Who am I, Lord,* or what is my calling, since you have worked in me with such divine power so that today I should regularly exalt and glorify your name wherever I happen to be not only when things go well but also in troubles, so that whatever may happen to me whether good or bad I am equally bound to accept it and always give thanks to God because he has shown that I should believe in him endlessly as trustworthy and he has taken notice of me so that in spite of my ignorance and [of our being] *in the last days* I should venture to undertake this task, good and wonderful as it is, in such a way that I should imitate those who the Lord had long ago foretold would declare his gospel *as a testimony to all nations* before *the end of the world,* and we see as a consequence that it has been fulfilled

33. 2 Chron.6:38; Rom. 8:11, 1 Cor. 2:11; Acts 2:29.   34. Ps. 94(95):9; Ps. 34(33):6, 7; 2 Sam. (2 Kgs.)7:18; Acts 2:17; Matt. 24:14.

barbed the attack made on Patrick by betraying his confidence concerning the sin. Patrick's emphasis on the publicity of his accusation suggests that it may have been made at an ecclesiastical synod. Two interesting points emerge from a consideration of this chapter: first, while his friend was canvassing for him Patrick was not in Britain. He could not possibly have been in Ireland. He must have been in Gaul. We shall return to this point later (see below, p. 113); second, the whole initiative for Patrick's being sent to Ireland came from Britain, not Gaul. It is quite certain that Patrick's "friend" was in Britain and that it was the British Church (not the Gallic nor the Roman Church) which launched the enterprise.

34. This chapter consists of one of those long loosely connected sentences in which Patrick seems to be thinking aloud. It brings out strongly his conviction that his evangelizing the Irish, the people at the end of the world, corresponds to his living in the last age of history. When the gospel will have been preached to every nation (and the Irish are the last on the list), then the world will end.

just so: you can see that we are witnesses that the gospel has been preached as far as the point where there is no one beyond.

IV / The Fruits of His Ministry in Ireland

35. But it is a long business to relate all my toil, whether individual incidents or parts of it. I will briefly tell how God who is most faithful often freed me from slavery and from twelve perils in which my life was endangered, as well as many plots and those things which I cannot describe in words. And I will not bore my readers; but I have God, who knows *everything* even *before it takes place*, as authority in that the divine Message frequently directed me even though I was a poor ignorant orphan.

36. *How did I come by this wisdom* which was not in me because *I did not know the number of my days*, nor used I to know God? Whence did this gift afterwards come to me, so great, so health-giving, the gift of knowing and loving God, but on condition that I should lose my country and kinsfolk?

37. I was even from time to time offered many gifts with weeping and tears, and I offended them, and also it was against the wish of some of my elders but by the providence of God I did not yield to them nor agree with them—no thanks to me, but it was God who prevailed in me and withstood them all, to enable me to come and preach the gospel to Irish tribes and endure insults from unbelievers, *to bear the reproach of my pilgrimage* and many persecutions, *even as far as being thrown into irons*, and to sacrifice my free status for the good of others, and, if I were worthy, I am ready [to give] my life unhesitatingly and willingly for his name and I want to sacrifice it there even if it involves death, if God were to kindly grant this to me.

35. Dan. 13:42 (Susanna 42).   36. Matt. 13:54; Ps. 38(39):5.   37. Ecclus. 29:30(23); 2 Tim. 2:9.

IV.35. We cannot descry in detail what these "twelve perils" were; they are not related one by one in this section of the work.

Patrick's description of himself as "a poor ignorant orphan" is of course an exaggeration. Most elderly people are orphans, but do not complain about it, and Patrick seems to have enjoyed his parents' company for some time after his return from captivity. But we are here witnessing the survival in Patrick's spirit of that deep trauma which his being kidnapped as an impressionable teenager inflicted on him. He never completely ceased to regard himself as a helpless, friendless victim of rapine.

37. Here Patrick is certainly referring to the period when he had been chosen by the British Church to go as a bishop to Ireland. His friends and relations tried to dissuade him. He returns to this theme in chapter 46. "Elders" here is the same word as the "seniors" of chapter 26 and probably refers either to the senior members of his tribe or extended family or to some of his ecclesiastical superiors (but not all, for most must have approved of his mission, otherwise he would hardly have gone).

38. Because I truly am a debtor to God, who gave me so much help that many people were reborn into God through me and afterwards were confirmed and that clergy were ordained everywhere for them, for a people who had recently come to belief whom the Lord chose *from the ends of the earth* as long ago *he had promised through his prophets: to you the nations will come from the ends of the earth and will say: just as our fathers took to themselves false idols and there is no usefulness in them,* and in another place, *I have set you as a light to the Gentiles so that you may be for their salvation even to the end of the earth.*

39. And I want to *await* his *promise* there, because of course he never deceives, just as he promises in the gospel, *They will come from east and west and will sit down with Abraham and Isaac and Jacob,* as we believe all believers will come from the whole world.

40. In consequence therefore we must of course fish well and steadily, just as the Lord warns us and teaches when he says: *Follow me and I will make you fishers of men*; and in another place he says through the prophets: *Look! I send fishers and many hunters, says God,* and so on. That is why we are strictly bound to spread out our nets, so that *an abundant multitude and a crowd* should be caught for God and that there should be clergy everywhere who should baptize and preach to the needy and expectant masses, just as the Lord says in the gospel, he warns and teaches in the text, *Go therefore now and teach all nations, baptizing them in the name of the Father and of the Son and of the Holy Spirit, teaching them to observe all things, whatever I have taught you.* And in another place he says, *Go therefore into the whole world and preach the gospel to every creature; whoever believes and is baptized will be saved but whoever does not believe will be damned.* And in another place: *This gospel of the Kingdom will be preached in the whole world as a testimony for all nations and then the end will come.* And in the same way the Lord foretells through the prophet in the text, *And it will come to pass in those days, says the Lord, I will pour out my Spirit*

38. Acts 13:47; Rom. 1:2, Jer. 16:19; Acts 13:47.   39. Acts 1:4; Matt. 8:11.   40. Matt. 4:19; Jer. 16:16; Luke 6:17, 5:6; Matt. 28:19–20; Mark 16:15–16, Matt. 24:14; Acts 2: 17–18 quoting Joel 2:28–29; Rom. 9:25–26 quoting Hos. 1:10, 2:1,24.

38. "Confirmed" here means the same as it does in *Letter* 2 (though Patrick uses a different word for it), that is, not only confirmed but admitted to communion. He uses the same word again with the same meaning in chapter 51. "Reborn" certainly means baptized.

40. This chapter is an enlargement of the theme touched on in *Letter* 11, and is only one of many resemblances between the two works which suggest that there cannot have been a great interval of time between their composition. Patrick piles text on text from the sacred book to establish his authority for working as a bishop in Ireland.

*upon all flesh and your sons and your daughters will prophesy and
your young men will see visions and your old men will dream dreams
and upon my menservants and upon my maidservants in those days
I will pour out my Spirit and they will prophesy.* And in Hosea he
says *I will call those who were not my people my people and her who
had not obtained mercy one who has obtained mercy and it will come
to pass in the place where it had been said: You are not my people,
there they will be called the sons of the living God.*

41. And so it is that those in Ireland who had never had knowledge
of God but up to now always only worshipped idols and filthy things,
how is it that recently a people of the Lord has been made perfect
and are called sons of God [and] the sons of the Irish and the daughters of subkings become monks and virgins of Christ?

42. There even was one blessed Irishwoman, an aristocrat of noble
race very beautiful and of full age, whom I baptized; and after a few
days for a particular reason she came to us, she indicated to us that
she had received a Message from an angel of God and he directed
her that she should become a virgin of Christ and that she should
draw closer to God: God be thanked, on the sixth day from that she
happily and eagerly chose that [career] which all the virgins of Christ
in the same way also choose—not with the consent of their fathers,
but they even endure persecutions and false accusations from their
relations and in spite of that their number continually increases (and
I cannot reckon the number from those of our race who have been
born there) apart from widows and people living a life of continence.
But those among them who are held in slavery have the hardest time:
they hold out steadfastly even against intimidation and threats; but

41. Patrick must have gained some support at least among local rulers if the children of petty kings were permitted to be converted and to take up the religious life, though we must discount the later traditions about his invariable success with the ruling classes in Ireland.

We have here unassailable evidence of Patrick's concern for the ascetic life. It is improbable that he was able to set up monasteries in which both male and female ascetics lived removed from the world, on the later model. What he encouraged was a manner of particularly strict life, lived according to vows voluntarily taken in the ordinary circumstances of the individual's life. See the comment on the next chapter.

Notice with what scorn and dislike Patrick speaks of the pagan religion of the Irish.

42. Patrick cannot conceal his pleasure that a member of the Irish nobility should have embraced an ascetic life, though he does not despise the lower orders when they do so.

"Those of our race" in all probability refers to people of British stock in Ireland, of whom there must have been a considerable number. No doubt they constituted the "Irish who believe in Christ" mentioned by Prosper. See Introduction, p. 12.

"Imitation" here means a determination to live a life of peculiar strictness, for the sake of Christ. Patrick uses it in the same sense again in *Confession* 47 and 59.

"Widows and people living a life of continence" refer respectively to women who have lost their first husbands and have taken a vow not to remarry and married couples who live together but as part of their Christian discipline refrain from sexual relations.

the Lord has given grace to many of his maidservants for even though they are forbidden still they steadfastly maintain their imitation [of Christ].

43. And so it is that even if I was willing to leave these women and make the journey to Britain—and I had been very willing for this because [it was] to my country and kinsfolk, and not that journey only but even as far as Gaul to visit the brothers and so that I should see the face of the holy ones of my Lord. God knows that I used to wish for it greatly, but I am *bound in the Spirit,* who *testifies* to me that if I shall have done this, he denounces me as destined to be found guilty and I am afraid of losing the results of the work which I have begun, and not I but the Lord Christ who commanded me that I should come to be with them for the rest of my life, if the Lord willed it and would guard me from every evil way, to prevent me sinning in his sight.

44. I hope that I ought to achieve this, but I do not trust myself *as long as I am in this body of death* because he is strong who daily strives to seduce me from my faith and the purity of a sincere religion which I have accepted for Christ my Lord to the end of my life. But the hostile flesh always draws me towards death, that is towards enticements unlawful to indulge in. And I *know in part* that I have not led the life of perfection as other believers have led it. But I profess to my Lord, and I am not ashamed in his sight, that I am not

43. Acts. 20:22–23.   44. 2 Pet. 1:13, Rom. 7:24; 1 Cor. 13:9.

43. Incoherence overtakes Patrick's Latin here also.

The reference to the possibility (which he discounts) that he might go to Gaul is interesting. We have already seen (above, on chapter 32) that it is virtually certain that he had at one time visited Gaul. The two classes of "brothers" and "holy ones" are not easy for us to distinguish, but it seems likely that they represent ordinary Christians on the one hand and monks on the other. Though it is possible, even probable, that monasticism in some form had reached Britain by Patrick's day, the nearest place where the fully developed monastic life would have been visible, and the source of inspiration for living an ascetic life, must in his day have been Gaul, where we know of monastic institutions existing in Lérins, Marseilles, Grincy, and Auxerre. At the same time it must be emphasized that the state of Patrick's Latin precludes the possibility of his having stayed for any long period in Gaul, as does the abundant evidence that his ecclesiastical training was received and his mission to Ireland supported in Britain.

Patrick's determination to remain in Ireland for the rest of his life is consistent with his silence about the presence of any fellow bishop with him in Ireland. He does not seem to have made any attempt to consecrate bishops. For this purpose he would have needed episcopal colleagues, and in his circumstances they were not easy to come by.

44. Patrick is not necessarily saying here that he has not led "the life of perfection" (which may mean one lived by some ascetic rule), but that he has not done so as well as others have.

lying: ever since I knew him from my youth up the love of God and fear of him has grown in me, and up to this day by the favor of the Lord *I have kept the faith*.

45. Let anyone laugh and revile me who wants to. I will not keep silence nor will I conceal the *signs and wonders* which have been shown me by the Lord many years before they took place, for he it is who knows everything *even before times eternal*.

46. And this is why I ought to thank God endlessly because he often pardoned my silliness and carelessness and that not only on one occasion, by not being fiercely angry with me, because I was appointed his assistant and yet I did not promptly fall in with what had been revealed to me and in accordance with what the *Spirit was prompting*, and the Lord *had pity on me a million times* because he saw in me that I had been ready. But as far as I was concerned in these circumstances I was not aware of what I should do about my situation, because many were disapproving of this mission, they even were talking among themselves behind my back and were saying, "Why is this fellow exposing himself to danger among enemies who do not know God?"—not because they were motivated by malice, but [the project] could not be understood by them because of my lack of education, as I have myself been confessing—and I did not quickly recognize the grace which was then in me. Now that which I ought [to have realized] has come home to me.

---

44. 2 Tim. 4:7.   45. Dan. 6:27; 2 Tim. 1:9.   46. John 14:26; Exod. 20:6.

45. One such "sign and wonder" shown long before could be the
dream described in *Confession* 23.

46. Here perhaps more than in any other passage Patrick's Latin
falls into incoherence and obscurity. The sentence beginning "But
as far as I was concerned" and ending "this mission" makes sense as
it is set down here, but the translation is largely guesswork. It is,
however, clear that Patrick is writing about the time when his going
as a missionary bishop to Ireland was in the balance, when his former
friend and later enemy was canvassing for him, when at least for part
of the time he was away in Gaul. There seem to have been several
different phases during this period: (1) When he was absent and his
friend was supporting his candidature; (2) When he had returned
and was at first uncertain whether he should go to Ireland or not;
whether this was before or after he had been formally chosen is uncertain, but if his friend announced the choice to him (perhaps immediately after his return from Gaul) we may guess that this phase
occurred after he had been chosen; (3) When he had decided that he
should go to Ireland but his friends and relations and even some of
his "seniors" opposed his decision and urged him not to go. Notice
that it was Patrick's lack of education that caused his hesitation. It is
worth noting, too, that Patrick explicitly says that those who opposed
his mission were not motivated by malice but by a mistaken desire
for his welfare. This distinguishes them sharply from the other, much
more serious, opponents who brought the grave accusation against
him, and confirms the conclusion that the occasion of the serious
attack was a quite separate one from the occasion when his mission
to Ireland was still in the balance.

The words used of the Irish by his well-meaning friends, "enemies
who do not know God," are far from complimentary, and make it
difficult to situate Patrick's home in any part of Britain (such as South

47. So now I have straightforwardly stated to my brothers and fellow servants in accordance with what I *foretold and still foretell* in order to strengthen and support your faith. I would like you to follow the way of imitation better and do more! This will be my boast because *a wise son is the boast of his father.*

48. *You know*, and God knows, *how* I have behaved myself since my youth in faithfulness to the truth and in sincerity of heart. I have also kept faith and will keep it with those tribes among whom I am living. God knows that *I took advantage of none* of them, and I do not intend to for the sake of God and his Church in case I should arouse persecution against them and against us all and in case the name of the Lord should be blasphemed through me, because it is written *Woe to the man through whom the name of the Lord is blasphemed.*

49. For though I am *unskilled in everything*, yet I tried to protect myself from the Christian brothers and the virgins of Christ and the devout women who used to give me voluntary gifts and they used to throw some of their personal jewelry on the altar and I used to give them back again to them and they used to be annoyed with me because I used to do this. But I [did it] because of the hope of the permanence [of my mission] to safeguard myself carefully in every way, for this very purpose that they should not catch me or the ministry of my service out in any charge of unfaithfulness and that I should not give an opportunity to the unbelievers for denigration or disparagement even in the smallest matters.

50. But perhaps when I baptized so many thousands of people I expected even half a farthing from one of them? *Tell me and I will repay you.* Or when the Lord ordained clergy everywhere through me, insignificant though I am, and I gave this ministry to them with-

47. 2 Cor. 13:2; Prov. 10:1.   48. Acts 20:18; 2 Cor. 7:2; Matt. 18:7, Rom. 2:24.   49. 2 Cor. 11:6.   50. 1 Sam. 12:3(VL).

Wales) where in the fifth century there were large numbers of Irish immigrants or settlers.

47. It is not easy to conjecture who these "brothers and fellow servants" were; perhaps Christians (and among them ascetics) in Britain; perhaps his converts in Ireland. The particular audience envisaged by Patrick varies throughout the *Confession*, but the Church in Britain is never far from his mind.

48–54. Patrick in these chapters defends himself in several ways against the charge of making his mission in Ireland a lucrative affair for himself. He certainly has in view here those in Britain who have been supporting his mission not only morally but also financially.

49. No money was minted in Ireland until at the earliest the ninth century, and no coin was produced in Britain for a long time, perhaps two centuries, after the year 410. Those who wished to give Patrick gifts could therefore only have rewarded him either with jewelry or with gifts in kind. Cattle in fact tended to be the currency in ancient Ireland.

The mention of the "altar" here is the only reference to anything directly to do with the eucharist in Patrick's works. But we have seen (above, p. 63) that for him confirmation, which he refers to several times, included admission to communion.

50. "Half a farthing" translates the name of a small leather coin, the *scriptula*, whose value had been reduced by the inflation of the third and fourth centuries to almost nothing.

out charge, if I exacted from any of them even the cost of a pair of shoes, *speak against me, and I will repay you*.

51. On the contrary *I incurred expense for* you in order that they should receive me and I used to travel among you and everywhere through many dangers even to outer areas beyond which there was nobody and where no one had ever penetrated who could baptize or ordain clergy or confirm the flock. By God's gift I achieved everything industriously and willingly for your salvation.

52. During this period I used to give presents to kings in addition to what I used to give as a salary to their sons who used to travel around with me, and in spite of that they arrested me with my companions and on that occasion they were very anxious to kill me, but my time had not yet come, and they stole whatever they found in our possession and they put me in irons, and on the fourteenth day the Lord freed me from their power and all our property was given back to us because of the Lord and the *close friends* which we had previously secured.

53. And you have experience of how much I paid out to those who administered justice in all the districts that I used to visit often. I reckon that I spent among them not less than the price of fifteen men, in order that you should enjoy me and I should always enjoy you in God. I do not regret it and it is not enough. *I am* still *spending and will spend to the limit*. The Lord is powerful enough to grant me later *to spend* myself *for your souls*.

50. 1 Sam. 12:3(VL).   51. 2 Cor. 12:15.   52. Acts 10:24.   53. 2 Cor. 12:15.

51. Patrick's reference to visiting areas where no one had ever before evangelized or ministered suggests strongly that there were other areas where people other than Patrick had penetrated as Christian missionaries. Patrick never claims to be the first Christian missionary in Ireland. It is therefore reasonable to assume that he knew of the activities of Palladius, the bishop sent by Pope Celestine in 431.

52. Why were the sons of kings traveling round with Patrick? One possible answer is that they guaranteed his safety, and his reference to being imprisoned in chains in spite of his giving presents to the kings' sons might support this view. Another theory is that he was instructing them, both in the Christian faith and also perhaps in reading and writing Latin.

The use by Patrick in the last few chapters of the imperfect tense, reproduced in the English translation, gives the distinct impression that he has been describing activities which he no longer carries on. In other words, Patrick is writing in semiretirement, at the very end of his life. The closing words of the *Confession* seem to confirm this conjecture.

53. "Those who administered justice" probably refers to the *brehons*, a class of men in Irish society who were learned in law, that is to say they were trained to carry in their heads the whole indiscriminate mass of law and lore, of custom and precedent and story and myth and religious ordinances by which the conduct of ancient Irish society was controlled. They did not in fact make the judicial decisions themselves, but were expert advisers to the kings or subkings who decided causes and cases.

"The price of fifteen men" gives us the standard of value observed in commercial or legal transactions, even though the currency must have been mainly calculated in cattle. The unit of value is probably not how much a slave would cost, but how much would have to be given in normal circumstances to compensate for the death or injury of a single man.

54. Now, *I call God as witness upon my soul that I am not lying*, and that I have not written to you *as an opportunity for flattery* or *greed*, and that I do not expect respect from any of you, for that respect is enough which is never seen but *is believed in the heart*. But he *who promised is faithful: he never tells lies*.

55. But I see that I have been promoted beyond measure by the Lord *in this present age*, and I was not worthy nor the kind of person to whom he might grant this, since I know for certain that poverty and disaster are more suitable for me than riches and luxury (but indeed the *Lord Christ was poor for our sakes*, but I am poor and unsuccessful and even though I were to desire riches I do not possess them, *nor do I judge myself*), because I daily expect either assassination or trickery or reduction to slavery or some accident or other, *but I fear none of these things on* account of the promises of heaven because I have thrown myself into the hands of Almighty God who reigns everywhere as the prophet says, *Cast your care upon the Lord and he will nourish you*.

V / Conclusion

56. So now *I commend my soul to* my *most trustworthy God* on whose *behalf I am carrying out a mission*, for all my humble status, but because he has no respect for persons he has even chosen me for this post that I should be *among his lowest* servants.

57. And that is why *I will pay him back for all that he has given to me*. But what shall I say or what promise shall I make to my Lord, because I have no power unless he will give it to me? But *let him search my heart and reins* because I am willing enough and more than enough and I have been prepared for him to grant me to *drink of his cup* as he has graciously allowed others among those who love him too.

54. 2 Cor. 1:23(VL), Gal. 1:20; 1 Thess. 2:5; Rom. 10:10; Heb. 10:23, Titus 1:12.   55. Gal. 1:4; 2 Cor. 8:9; 1 Cor. 4:3; Acts 20:24; Ps. 55(54): 22(23).   56. 1 Pet. 4:19; Eph. 6:20; Matt. 25:40.   57. Ps. 116(115):11(12); Ps. 7:9(10); Matt. 20:22.

V.57 The reference at the end of this chapter to people who have endured martyrdom could of course be taken to refer to the martyrs of the British Church, Alban and Aaron and Julius. But it equally could refer to those who had been martyred in Ireland, for martyrdom in Ireland is the fate which Patrick desired (though as far as we know he did not attain it). If this were so, it would throw some faint light on the otherwise obscure fate of bishop Palladius. Patrick seems to be referring to the same people in chapter 59.

58. Consequently may it never happen from my God that I should ever lose *his people which he has gathered* in the ends of the earth. I pray God that he may grant me perseverance and graciously allow me to bear him faithful witness until my passing for the sake of my God.

59. And if I ever practiced this imitation with any success for the sake of my God, whom I love, I ask him that he may grant that I may spill my blood along with those [other] exiles and prisoners even though I may lack burial itself or my corpse may be most squalidly torn limb from limb by dogs or wild beasts or *the birds of the air may devour it.* I believe most confidently that if this were to happen to me I have gained my soul along with my body, because, without a shadow of doubt, on that Day *we shall rise* in the radiance of the sun, that is *in the glory* of Christ Jesus our Redeemer, as *children of the living God* and *coheirs with Christ and destined to be conformed to his image,* because we shall reign *from him and through him and in him.*

60. For the sun which we see rises every day for our benefit at his behest, but it will never reign nor will its radiance endure, but all who worship it will come to a bad end in wretched punishment as well. But we who believe in and adore the true sun, Christ, who will never die, nor will anyone die *who has done* his *will,* but *he will last for ever just as Christ lasts for ever,* Christ who reigns with God the Father almighty and with the Holy Spirit before ages and now and for all ages of ages. Amen.

61. Now, once again I will briefly set out the words of my Confession: *I testify* in truth and in exultation of heart *before God and his*

---

58. Isa. 43:21.   59. Luke 8:5; 1 Cor. 15:43; Rom. 8:16, 17, 29; Rom. 11:36.   60. 1 John 2:17 (VL).   61. 2 Tim. 4:1; 1 Tim. 5:21.

59–60. In these two chapters Patrick, who has earlier recorded for us a curious dream experience which he had in connection with the rising sun (see above, on chapter 20), goes out of his way to repudiate sun-worship. Christ was often represented in early Christian art as the true sun: one can recall among many other examples the early fourth-century mosaic in the pre-Constantinian necropolis under the basilica of St. Peter in Rome depicting Christ as the sun god, with rays streaming from a halo round his head, ascending the sky in his horse-drawn chariot. Patrick's words in this chapter reflect this particular cult. But his allusion to sun-worship among the heathen Irish is interesting, because in fact evidence for sun-worship among the Celts is sparse. The Celts did not directly associate their gods with particular exclusive activities, such as war or learning or healing, as the Greeks and Romans did. There are however enough small pieces of evidence that the cult of the sun was not unknown among the Celts to make this reference by Patrick not extraordinary or eccentric. It also reflects once more his violent repudiation of paganism.

60–62. The resemblance in form of the conclusion of the *Confession* to the conclusion of the *Letter* has been observed. Both include a reference to the three Persons of the Trinity. Both have a liturgical-sounding formula ending with Amen not at the end but just before the end. This is yet another sign that the writing of the *Confession* cannot have been long removed in time from that of the *Letter*.

holy angels that I have never had any motive apart from his gospel and promises to return to that nation from which I was only just able to escape.

62. But I beg those who believe in God and fear him whoever shall condescend to peruse or to receive this writing which Patrick, a very badly educated sinner, has written in Ireland, that nobody shall ever say that it was I, the ignoramus, if I have achieved or shown any small success according to God's pleasure, but you are to think and it must be sincerely believed, that it was the gift of God. And this is my Confession before I die.

62. As he composes a carefully planned finale, Patrick is unable to exclude from it two more references to that lack of education which obsessed him throughout his career. It is however a moving final statement, reflecting Patrick's entirely genuine humility and concluding with the immense dignity of the words "This is my confession before I die." It was indeed his writings, and his *Confession* particularly, which kept the memory of Patrick green. For nearly two centuries after his death there is no reference to him in any surviving literature. But his *Confession* and his *Letter* were being preserved and copied somewhere during that obscure period, waiting for the moment when the politics of the Irish Church would find his a useful name to revive.

Recommended Reading

Bury, J. B. *Life of St. Patrick*. London, 1905.

O'Rahilly, T. F. *The Two Patricks*. Dublin, 1942.

Chadwick, Norah, ed. *Studies in the Early British Church*. Cambridge, 1958.

Binchy, D. A. *St. Patrick and His Biographers. Studia Hibernica* 2 (1962) pp. 1–173.

Dillon, M., ed. *Early Irish Society*, 2d ed. Dublin: 1963.

Barley, M. W. and Hanson, R. P. C., eds. *Christianity in Britain 300–700*. Leicester, 1968.

Hanson, R. P. C. *St. Patrick: His Origins and Career*. Oxford, 1968.

Hughes, Kathleen. *Early Christian Ireland*. London, 1972.

Thomas, C. *Christianity in Roman Britain to* A.D. *500*. London, 1981.

Index
of
Biblical References

Index
of
Names and Subjects